M000305688

IMAGES
of America

LURAY *and*
PAGE COUNTY

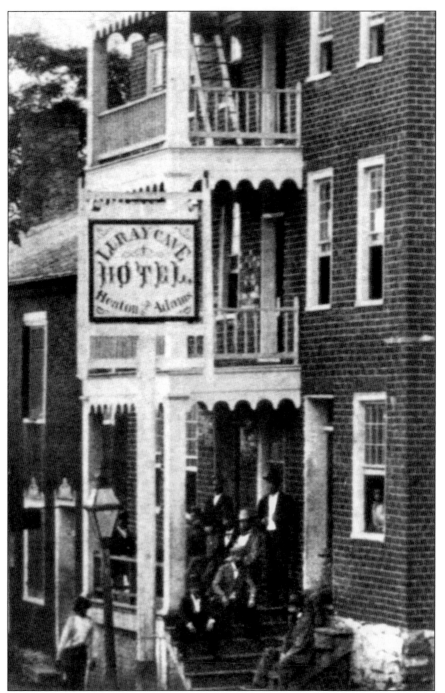

The initial discovery of Luray Caverns prompted a flurry of activity. In July 1880, Benton P. Stebbins, co-discoverer of the caverns, took this photograph of a Smithsonian exploration party in front of the Luray Cave Hotel. They had arrived in New Market and decided to visit Endless Caverns as well but were denied entry when the owner, Rueben Zirkle, stated he had never heard of the Smithsonian Institution. (Copyrighted photo courtesy of *Discovery of Luray Caverns, Virginia* by Russell H. Gurnee.)

IMAGES
of America

LURAY *and*
PAGE COUNTY

Dan Vaughn

ARCADIA

Published by Arcadia Publishing
Charleston SC, Chicago IL, Portsmouth NH, San Francisco CA

Printed in Great Britain

Library of Congress Catalog Card Number: 2004114041

For all general information contact Arcadia Publishing at:
Telephone 843-853-2070
Fax 843-853-0044
E-mail sales@arcadiapublishing.com
For customer service and orders:
Toll-Free 1-888-313-2665

Visit us on the internet at http://www.arcadiapublishing.com

This book is in honor of my parents, Ann and Glendon Vaughn, on the occasion of their 50th wedding anniversary, June 8, 2005.

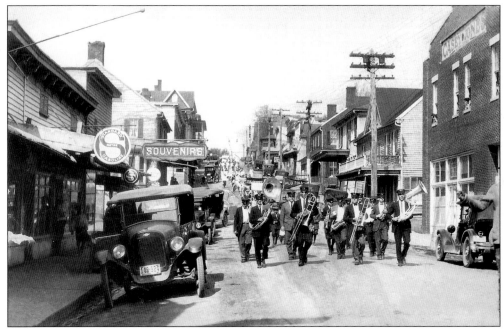

In 1912, one of the annual big events was the school rally day. Many Page County schools converged for a parade of pageantry on Main Street in Luray. Seen here, in front of the Mud Pike School class, is Isaac Coffman, left trombone player of the Luray Cornet Band. D.L. Kauffman's Jewelry Souvenir Store is at far left. (C.R. and Diane Griffith Collection.)

CONTENTS

ACKNOWLEDGMENTS

I am grateful to a number of people who assisted me in bringing this book to print. I am most appreciative of the staff at Arcadia Publishing, especially my editor, Kathryn Korfonta, for her encouragement and guidance. A special thank you goes to the *Page News and Courier* staff of Patti Burner, Bonita Deavers, editor Jeb Caudill—who allowed me free reign of the archive— and Deloris Judy, whose tireless compilations of decades' worth of the paper's "Yesteryears" column became a large portion of the reference framework that this pictorial hinged on. Thanks also go to David Breneman for his exhaustive editing work and Ed "Casey" Billhimer, of the Elkton Historical Society, for his willingness to freely share images and information—a true preservationist. Rod Graves, of the Luray Caverns Corporation, openly shared from that organization's archives, and Debbie Owens extensively searched historical Page County reference materials. I also want to thank the following institutions for their generosity in permitting the use of their archival material: Virginia Historical Society, Virginia Tech Special Collections, Virginia Department of Historical Resources, Library of Virginia, George Eastman House (Rochester), Page Public Library, Bridgewater College, O. Winston Link Museum, Norfolk Southern Corporation, and the Norfolk and Western Historical Society. The following individuals were also helpful, and I am indebted to their graciousness: Karen Cooper, Becky George, Irvin Judd Jr., Lloyd Kibler, Debbie McDonough, Karen Miller, Kim Pulice, Ruth Reid, Allan Rinaca, Jimmy Rinker, Ben Ritter, Nick Smith, Warren and Penny Smith, Charles Stevens, Patty Temple, the Town of Stanley, Brandon Vaughn, Jordan Vaughn, and Josh Vaughn.

INTRODUCTION

When inventor, painter, and budding photographer Samuel F.B. Morse, at the announcement of photography's birth in 1839, said, "We shall have rich material . . . an exhaustless store for the imagination to feed on," he had already realized the visual access to the past this would create.

Page County had been established just eight years prior to that statement, but formal petitions to the Commonwealth's government had begun as early as 1792. The very first issue of the Woodstock *Herald*, of December 24, 1817, carried this note in "Extracts from the journal of the House of Delegates for December 8th": "A variety of petitions were read—among those one from sundry citizens of part of Shenandoah and Rockingham counties, praying the formation of a new county." Citizens had petitioned the state for their own county because the long trip across the Massanutten Mountain to Woodstock, Shenandoah's county seat, was too cumbersome. Fourteen years later, these pleas were answered, and by an act of the Virginia General Assembly on March 30, 1831, Page County was established. The county seat was fixed at Luray, which had been established on August 12, 1812, in what was then Shenandoah County. Approximately three-fourths of Page was carved from Shenandoah County, with Rockingham County contributing from its northeast corner the remainder of what is Page County. Page was originally part of Charles River County, now York, one of the eight shires into which Virginia was divided in 1634 by the General Assembly, then in Jamestown.

The new county had been named by Col. John Gatewood of Luray to honor John Page, who had served as lieutenant governor of Virginia during the American Revolution and later as a member of the First U.S. Congress, as well as Virginia's governor from 1802 to 1805.

Small communities dotted Page County, with most containing a store, church, school, flour mill, post office, blacksmith shop, and a not-too-distant depot and with names such as Valleyburg, Carlotta, Santiago, and East Liberty. These were but just a few of the mountain and river communities and flagstops on the Shenandoah Valley Railroad.

Ruffner's Cave, on Cave Hill, was known about since 1795 but did not compare to what the discoverers would find on the afternoon of August 13, 1878. With news of this magnificent discovery, the lingering completion of the Shenandoah Valley Railroad now took precedence. Hundreds, even thousands, came daily by train and stagecoach to see this natural wonder. The first automobile ever seen in Luray came in October 1900, bringing tourists from Washington City. Luray's attraction made it world-famous almost overnight, and the residents of this quaint valley town had to adjust to the large numbers of new visitors. Prof. Jerome J. Collins, the explorer and *New York Herald* correspondent, postponed his North Pole expedition to extensively research the caverns. Unfortunately, he later perished when he resumed his arctic venture, the caverns being his last completed assignment.

With the continuing advancement of the railroad towards Page from both Hagerstown in the north and Basic City—present-day Waynesboro—in the south, railroad company officials had sought a location to construct their divisional workshops. The small village of Port Republic, Virginia, was approximately at the center, but local landowners concerned over labor issues would deny the railroad the opportunity to build there. They would instead build further north, at Milnes—present-day Shenandoah. Port Republic's loss was Page County's gain—for a season. The construction from both directions culminated in Luray, and the two rails were connected on March 24, 1881. Economically speaking, this was probably the greatest event in the history of Page County. Full operations of the railroad began, and the first train passed through Luray on April 18, 1881.

Even though the name Stanley was accepted by the people as early as 1884 and incorporated by the Virginia General Assembly on Valentine's Day 1900, it would be 11 years later before it could officially be used as a postal address. The South Stanley Land and Improvement Company had been established to divide parcels of land, and James McNider, president of the Stanley Furnace and Land Company, played a key role in its development. The town would ultimately be named after his favorite nephew, Stanley McNider. The Page Valley Academy and the Valley View Seminary both operated in Stanley for a short period in the 1890s.

When Page County was established in 1831, there were 24 merchant flour mills in operation. The newly implemented roller process was taking precedence over the old burr method of producing flour, and by 1900, most mills had converted to steam power. Ultimately though, the mill itself would fall victim to progress, with just a handful remaining today. In the late 1800s and early 1900s, there were also many small weekly newspapers in Page, and they started, flourished, died, restarted, consolidated, and changed names and owners frequently. More than 15 Page County newspapers would vanish or combine into our present *Page News and Courier*. The consolidation of public education would also render the more than 70 small, one-room schoolhouses obsolete, and so it was with post offices in Page County as well, when they would start to be discontinued at the onset of the Rural Free Delivery's initiation. Seemingly, the biggest change of all was the separation of the people from the railroad, when local passenger rail service was discontinued, and each community's depot was removed. This was hard for the citizens to accept. The town of Shenandoah was hardest hit when its rail shops were discontinued in the late 1950s. The face of the county was changing, and many times the only remnant was a photograph of an event or a structure now gone forever.

If a picture is truly worth a thousand words, when one takes a closer look, it may be that half of those words are additional questions. Seeing a time or place perhaps you never knew existed inspires wonder. Thoughts are juxtaposed with a different era, envisioning all that was happening within each photograph. It was a quaint and long-ago world, with a way of life that seems far removed and out of place in our current society, and the works of the photographers are now treasures.

An exhaustive effort was made to ascertain the information and facts contained herein. Images of America: *Luray and Page County* is by no means intended to be a thorough pictorial or reference history but rather an effort to broadly capture a bygone era in photographic print that began in this quiet county over 120 years ago.

Dan Vaughn
Luray, Virginia

One
THE PUBLIC REALM

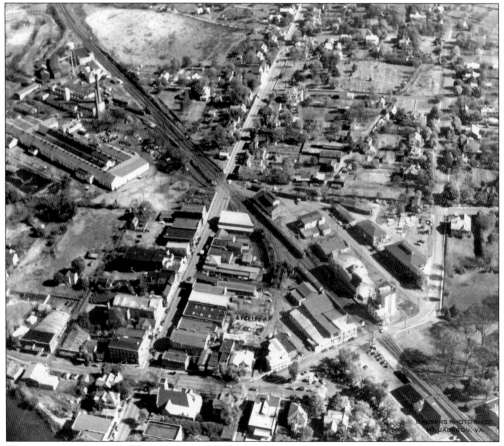

This interesting aerial of Luray, taken by Garbers Photo Shop of Mount Jackson around 1950, shows a multitude of businesses and industries in the town. (Dan Vaughn Collection.)

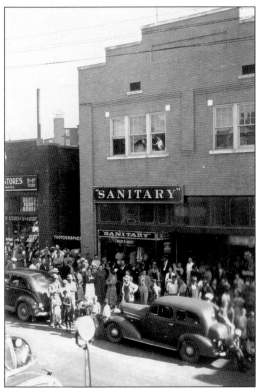

This late 1930s photo shows the Sanitary Market, a popular grocery store in Luray that had opened in 1932. Luray Pancake and Buckwheat Flour, both made by local Page Milling Co., were sold exclusively in all Sanitary Stores throughout the country. Being acquired in the late 1930s, the Sanitary name would continue in Luray through the 1950s, when they then took on their parent name Safeway. (Lloyd Kibler Collection.)

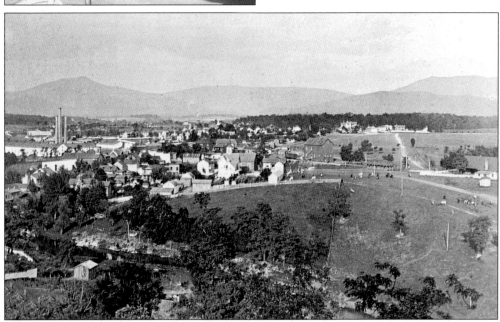

This rare glass plate positive shows a quaint Luray in a time when cattle grazed freely around the town. Some of the structures shown in this c. 1895 view are Deford Tannery at left, Mt. Carmel Baptist Church in center, C.W. Carter's flour mill right of center, the original Shenandoah Valley Railroad passenger station further right, and at far right is the Luray Inn Restaurant, the inn having burned just before this image. (Virginia Historical Society Collection.)

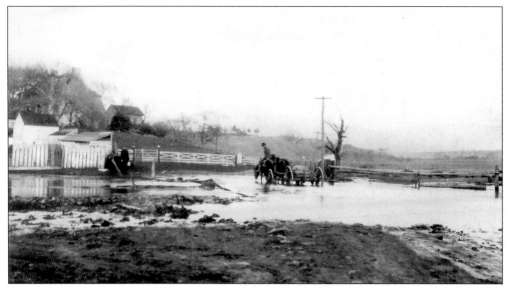

Posing for a photographer halfway through the ford to Spring Farm at the turn of the last century, the horse in this picture takes advantage of the opportunity for a drink of fresh water from Hite's Spring. This spring remains as a source of water for the town of Luray. (St. George's Episcopal Church Collection.)

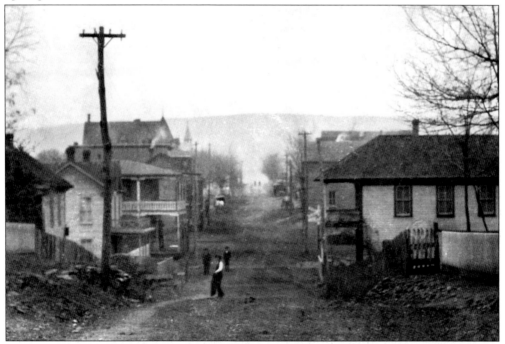

In 1885, a small town in Henry County, Virginia, called Stanley, would have first rights to this name, and in that community the town was quite commonly referred to as Stanley Town. In a strange twist of irony, to alleviate confusion, the Henry County and Page County towns actually exchanged names in 1911: Stanleyton became Stanley, and the Henry County community became Stanleytown, a name that it had already unintentionally assumed. (Ed "Casey" Billhimer Collection.)

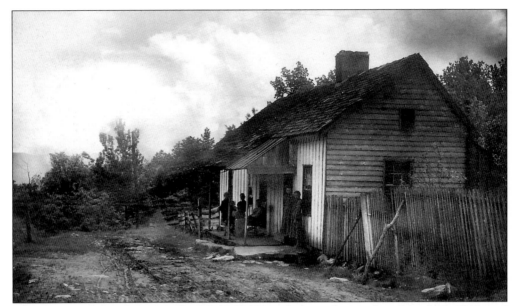

The New Market and Sperryville (NM&S) Turnpike was chartered on March 6, 1848, and constructed by contractor Emanuel Grove in 1849. In January 1894, the *Page Courier* stated, "This is by far the most important highway in the county." Shown is the tollhouse and gate on the east side of the White House Bridge, with Mr. T.C. Strickler as gatekeeper, while another tollgate was in East Luray. A toll of 10¢ was collected for horse-drawn vehicles. (Gerald W. Painter Collection.)

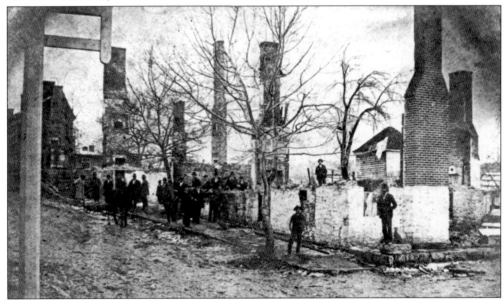

Photographer James H. Bushong, along with William Campbell—who would shortly co-discover Luray Caverns—took this January 1877 photograph of the burnt district of West Main Street in Luray. The fire was a setback to the town, especially with Reconstruction in its early stages. Among the businesses destroyed were the Modesitt and Union Hotels. The Luray Inn would fill this void when built in 1881. (Copyrighted photo courtesy of *Discovery of Luray Caverns, Virginia* by Russell H. Gurnee.)

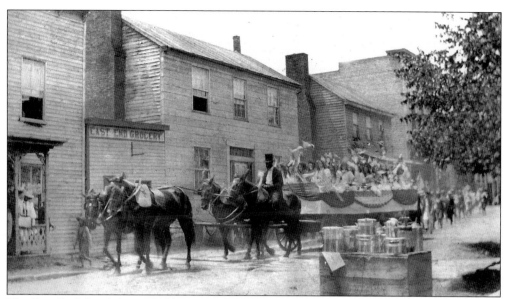

The East End Confederate Soldier Monument, erected by local sculptor Herbert Barbee, was dedicated on July 21, 1898, to coincide with the Battle of First Manassas. The procession started at the monument, marched west, and is seen here returning for the ceremonies. Deford Tannery had initially donated a triangular lot to the town at the intersection of the Shenandoah Valley Railroad and the NM&S Turnpike, with Barbee's acceptance to stand the monument there. It never happened. (Dan Vaughn Collection.)

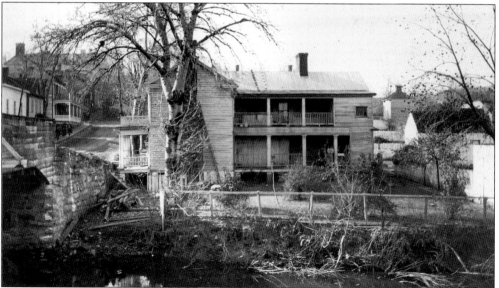

This rare glass plate image, taken in November 1895 by Charles Pancoast, shows a portion of the old wood-and-rock bridge on West Main Street in Luray. In 1842, the Page County Court had ordered Daniel Blosser to "bridge the Hawksbill by building a wooden pen between the abutments and filling it with rock." Currently, Brown's Restaurant is located where the house is shown. The bridge was tested in July 1889, when four large elephants and a host of other circus animals passed over it, their combined weight being over 10 tons. (George Eastman House Collection.)

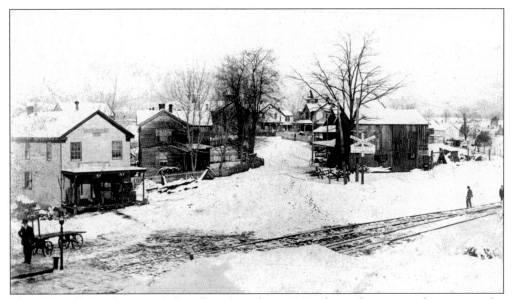

This view of Main Street in Rileyville, taken about 1920, shows the center of town near the Norfolk and Western (N&W) Railroad. The Hugh Wood and Bob Abbott General Store is shown at left; next to the store is George Keyser's house, formerly the Rileyville Post Office. At right behind the railroad sign is Ed Culler's Blacksmith Shop. The unidentified man at far left stands beside the kerosene lantern at the Rileyville Depot platform. (Karen Cooper Collection.)

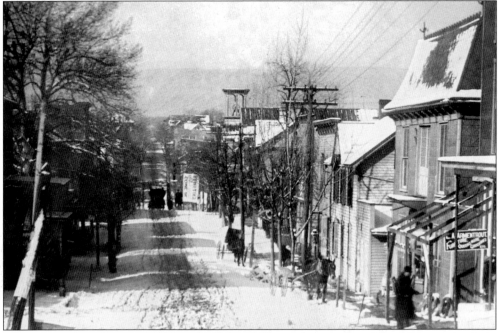

This was a typical snowy day in the late 1890s on Luray's East Main Street. An L.A. Armentrout sign reads "Furniture, Queensware, Groceries, Etc." Further west, Grove and Bro. hangs a street banner advertising "Bargains, Come In." Electricity has come full force, but the old kerosene street lamps remained. Stover's acetylene gas lamps were installed before Edison's "gas light in a bottle" lit Luray. (Becky George Collection.)

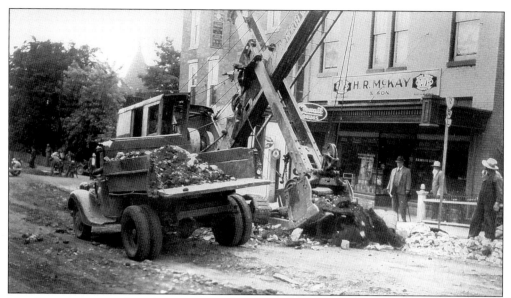

Metalling, a process of coating a street with quartzite because of its hardness and resistance to forming ruts, had become somewhat primitive. In the spring of 1895, the Town of Luray, considering macadamizing the streets, bought a rock crusher capable of producing 100 tons of macadam a day. The dust created was inconvenient and unbearable, so the town paved many of its busy streets with asphalt in the 1930s. (Lloyd Kibler Collection.)

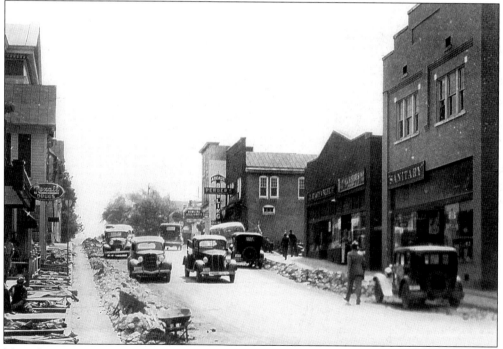

Main Street Luray was growing, and pedestrian walkways made of tan bark and even crushed limestone were outdated materials for the merchant trade to have tracked into their stores. Sidewalk superintendents were on hand this day, in 1937, to oversee the beginning of the change to concrete. (Lloyd Kibler Collection.)

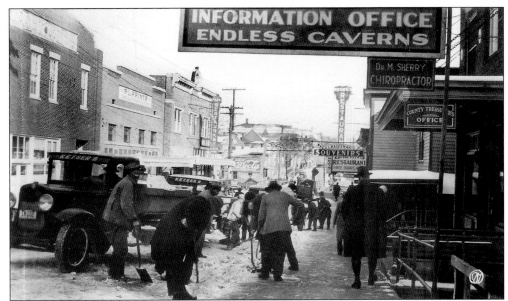

This Civil Works Administration (CWA) project had a street cleaning crew busy on this snowy February day in 1934, with Luray town manager Leath R. Renalds, at far right, testing out their work. The Page County Treasurer's Office was then located on West Main Street. With the number of tourists flowing to Luray, the Endless Caverns of New Market would open an auxiliary office among the potential market that Main Street in Luray was offering. (Bridgewater College Archives Collection.)

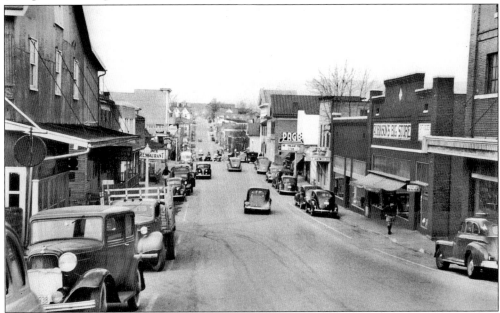

Henry Robinson opened his Robinson Brothers store, seen at right, in Luray on August 1, 1922, and it came to be a well-known establishment on East Main Street. In 1937, it became Robinson's Big Store. It was sold in 1965. Also seen in this 1940s photograph, from left to right, are Moyer Bros. Coal, Tom's Restaurant, Parkway Shell, Page Theater, and Earl's Sandwich Shop. (Millie Gochenour Collection.)

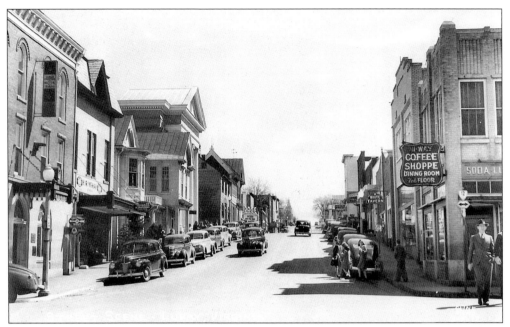

This was East Luray, from the First National Bank to the Highway Coffee Shoppe. This is where Route 12—present-day U.S. Route 340—made its crossing. Ironically, Page County had temporarily "loaned" the Route 340 designation that it was originally assigned in 1933 to Winchester, Virginia. It only became Route 12 from 1937 to 1954, when the county would again resume the familiar route number. (Ann Vaughn Collection.)

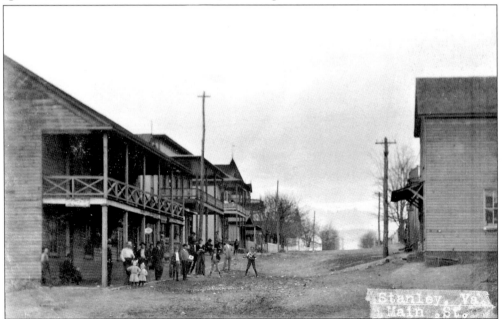

Stanley, having its earliest origins as Marksville Station, Virginia, is where the New Market and Gordonsville Turnpike intersected with the Shenandoah Valley Railroad. In this 1909 photograph, a disaster was just waiting to happen—all the structures east of the turreted house would be consumed by fire. (Town of Stanley Collection.)

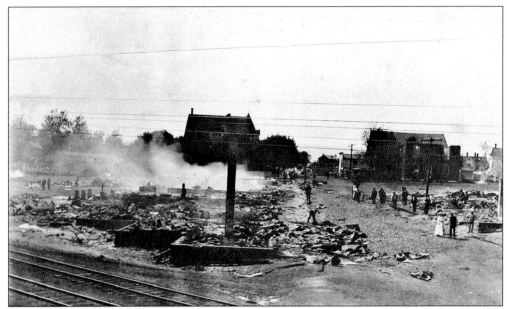

The most disastrous fire in the history of Page County occurred here on May 4, 1909, resulting in the destruction of practically the entire town. Sixteen buildings were destroyed, including Grim's Hotel, Stanleyton Post Office (all mail was saved), D.M. Modesitt Dry Goods, Stanley Milling Company, Stanley Produce Company, C.B. Foote Hardware, the storehouses of Shryock and Mauck, Berrey and Landram, T.M. Keyser, B.M. Shenk, R.J. Hamrick, Mrs. Varner's dwelling and stable, and other warehouses. (Town of Stanley Collection.)

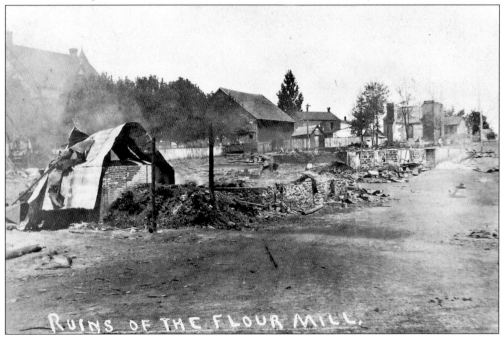

The fire started when trash being burned on a windy day at the Stanley Milling Company got out of control. Catching the mill on fire, the blaze spread until it crossed Main Street. As seen in this image, only the rock foundation remained. (Town of Stanley Collection.)

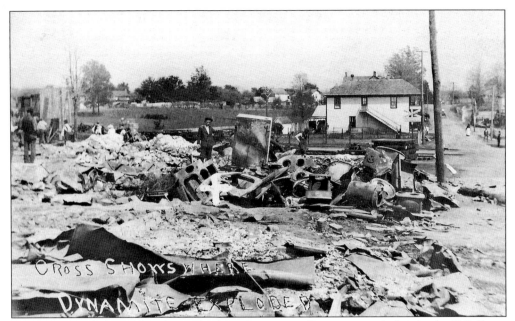

This photograph shows the aftermath of the destruction. Dynamite exploding in the C.B. Foote General Merchandise Store did not help matters. Mr. Foote was familiar with loss, though: in an earlier Stanley fire of August 1894, his store was one of seven buildings destroyed. He had previously occupied a storehouse across Main Street. Relocating did not help, but he was heavily insured this time. (Town of Stanley Collection.)

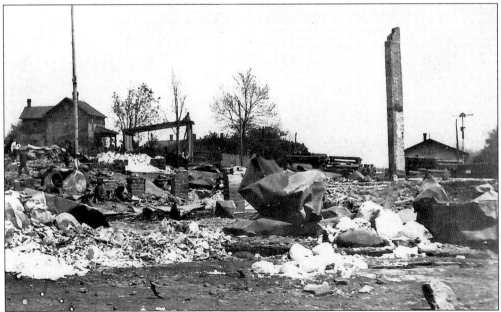

This postcard image taken by Wallace Rhodes, a Federal Trade Commission photographer, was mailed only 22 days after the fire. The downtown section was destroyed, except for the brick Stanley Hotel and the house of Irene Offenbacker. Contrary to popular belief, the Stanley Depot, as seen on the right, did not burn in this fire but did burn later that year in an unrelated incident on November 16, 1909, and yet again in December 1917. (Town of Stanley Collection.)

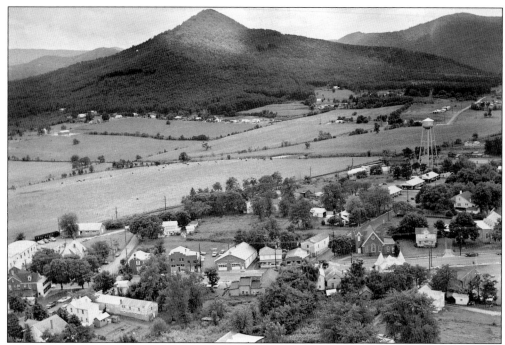

This quaint view of Stanley, photographed in the late 1960s, shows Roundhead Mountain in the background. The Judy Lane expansion was in its early stages, and the town had just received its new post office. Farmland continued to predominantly surround the town, but renewal was about to take place. (Aubrey D. Foltz Collection.)

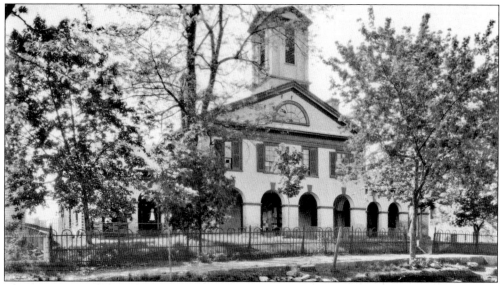

The Page County Courthouse was completed on December 23, 1833, at a cost of $6,000. Arriving late for session, Enos McKay compensated the court with a bell. Architects Malcolm F. Crawford and William B. Philips, who designed the structure, incorporated a steeple for the bell. For safekeeping, court records were stored in a cave outside Luray during the Civil War. When found damaged by water, many were recopied. The courthouse was occupied by both armies. (Virginia Historical Society Collection.)

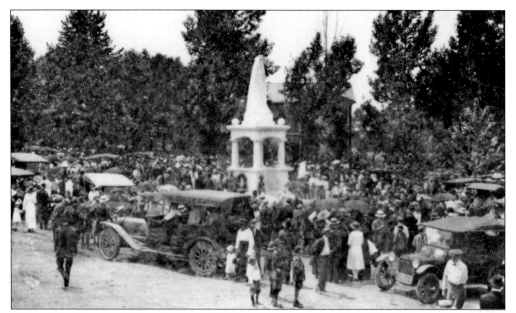

When John Beatty Siebert Jr. unveiled this monument on July 20, 1918, there was great fanfare in Luray. Although frequently attributed to Luray sculptor Herbert Barbee, who produced the East End Confederate Soldier Monument, the Broad Street granite statue was actually carved by sculptors hired by the McNeil Marble Company of Marietta, Georgia. (Marleen Hansen Collection.)

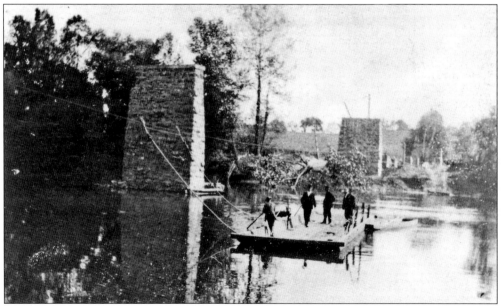

In 1899, an ice freshet caused the White House Bridge ferryboat to wash downstream with operator William Price, seen here in a 1906 photograph, and his son Charley on board. The latter jumped off, saying, "There are more pines than Charley Prices." Piers, still standing from the 1870 Flood, would linger for over 40 years before the bridge would be rebuilt. An earlier bridge was intentionally burned by Federal troops under Gen. T.J. "Stonewall" Jackson to keep the Union Army at bay. (Virginia Historical Society Collection.)

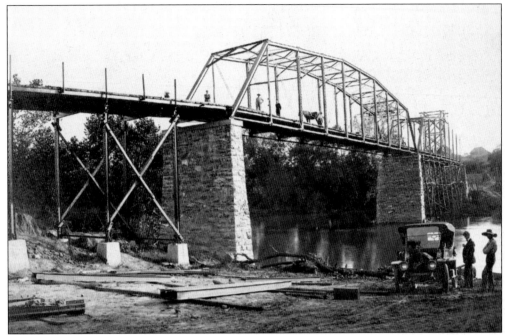

This photograph by the Frensley Studio shows the fourth bridge to span the Shenandoah at White House Crossing, completed on October 1, 1914. Built of iron, it was still standing when the fifth and current bridge opened in 1947. A series of three wooden covered bridges, two of which had previously been built approximately 300 yards south, were destroyed by wind, fire, and rain, respectively. (Ed "Casey" Billhimer Collection.)

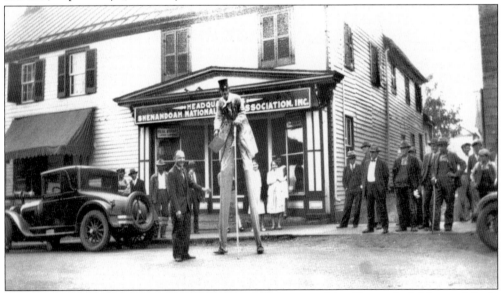

L. Ferdinand Zerkel was instrumental in the establishment of the Shenandoah National Park. Park headquarters were located on West Main Street in Luray until a permanent structure could be erected. The exterior weatherboarding was later removed to expose the familiar logs of this structure, which housed the popular Luray Museum opening in May 1938. (Shenandoah National Park Archives, L. Ferdinand Zerkel Collection.)

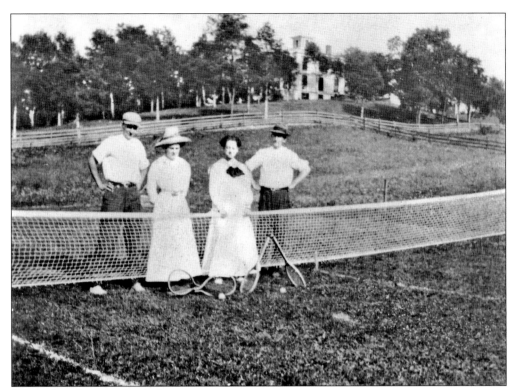

When this photograph of a lawn tennis court was taken on Aventine Hill in 1906, there were already three courts in Luray. Seen in the background is the old Peter Borst mansion, removed to South Court Street in the 1930s, and Mimslyn Inn, now residing in its place. Note the tennis outfits of the day. (Virginia Historical Society Collection.)

The Luray Singing Tower, designed by J. Raymond Mims and officially known as the Belle Brown Northcott Memorial, was dedicated before a crowd of 5,000 on November 13, 1937, with Anton Brees as its first carillonneur. Built of native Massanutten sandstone, the campanile was, along with an endowment, a gift to the town of Luray by Col. T.C. Northcott and his daughter, Mrs. Katherine Northcott Graves. (Warren and Penny Smith Collection.)

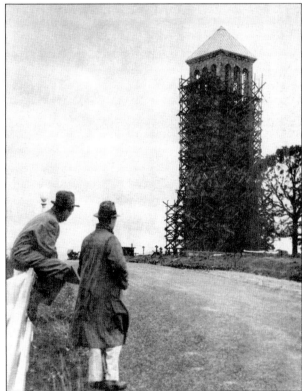

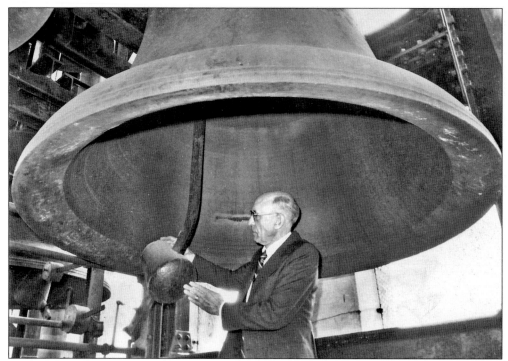

Cast in bronze by the Taylor Bell Foundry of Loughborough, England, this 7,640-pound, 6-foot-wide bell, the largest of 47, has an inscription that reads, "Glory to God, Peace on Earth, Good Will to Men." In October 1937, J. Maurice Grove of Luray hauled the 36,170 pounds of bells to a near-completed carillon with his Spotswood Transfer Company. The bells, bolted to steel beams and not actually moving, are struck by the clappers. (Dan Vaughn Collection.)

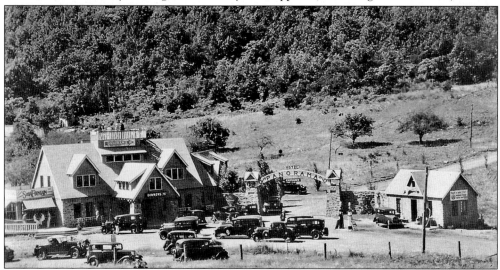

This mountaintop resort, opening on July 20, 1924, was popularized with the advent of the automobile. It became a full-service stop with food, lodging, auto service, and even snow cones. With dinner and a view for 75¢, it could not be passed up. Managed by J. Allen Williams of Luray, Panorama was named for the nearby home of noted sculptor William Randolph Barbee. (Dan Vaughn Collection.)

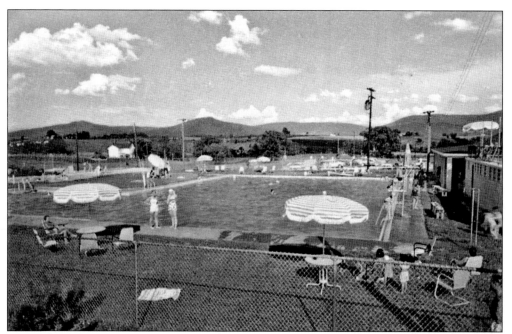

For over 30 years, swimming in Woodland Park Pool was a favorite summertime activity in Luray. When the pool's first swim meet was held on May 30, 1954, cottage rentals, tennis, and shuffleboard were also offered. It would close in 1987, and the clubhouse was intentionally burned. (Dan Vaughn Collection.)

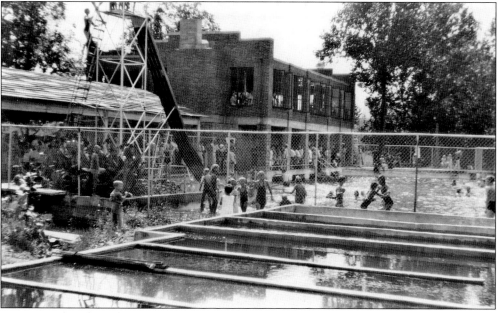

First opened to the public in 1931, Shuler's Pool became a popular summertime site. Naturally fed by mountain water filtered through a series of troughs, the pool could generally be expected to offer cold swimming. Shortly after its opening, owner Harry Shuler had a high sliding board installed, and it was so popular that a second, smaller slide was erected alongside. Purchased by the Town of Stanley in 1992, it is still in operation. (Dan Vaughn Collection.)

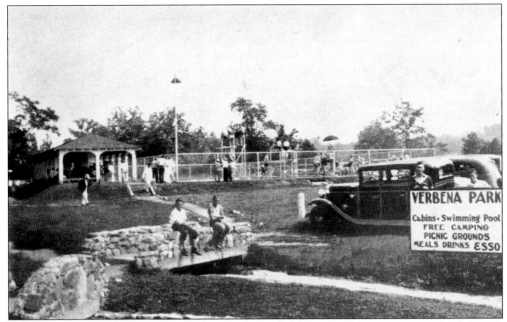

Verbena Park, developed by the Hisey brothers of Shenandoah, was built adjacent to the Verbena Mills in 1935. It was a popular recreational area, operated by Floyd and Anne Stanley, featuring a dining room and rental cabins on a 25-acre park. The Verbena Post Office had its origins in the extinct Rockingham County community of Waverlie. (Ed "Casey" Billhimer Collection.)

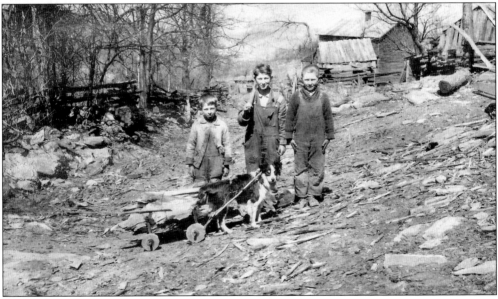

Pictured from left to right are Dan Thomas, Simon Offenbacker, and Simon's brother, Lloyd, of Tanner's Ridge, using a dog-powered wagon to get this job done. Wood was the staple of the day, being used for heating, cooking, building, and even wagon wheels. Their walking sticks are probably lying just beyond the camera's lens as well. This 1920s view shows a Page County before the formation of the Shenandoah National Park. (St. George's Church Collection.)

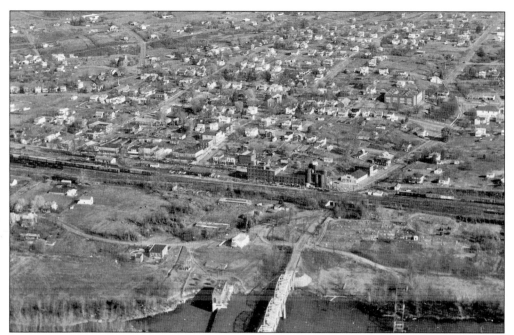

This mid-1950s aerial photograph of Shenandoah shows a broad view of business and activity in Page County's southernmost town. The old 1890 bridge, once collecting tolls, is still standing. Its dismantling became an issue because of the cost, and it would stand unused for almost 20 years before being razed by the Dean Excavating Company of Elkton, Virginia. Shenandoah Flour Mills, at center, was Page County's largest mill at one time. (Irvin Judd Jr. Collection.)

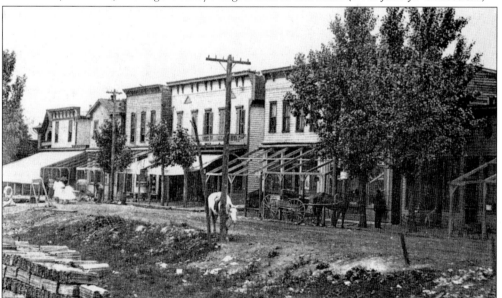

First Street—or Front Street as it came to be known, as it fronted the railroad—continued to be the "main" street of Shenandoah into the late 1950s because of the railroad activity there. There were a variety of stores with all the necessities of the day. The horse in this photograph, taken around 1905, seems oblivious to its surroundings. (*Shenandoah: A History of Our Town and Its People.*)

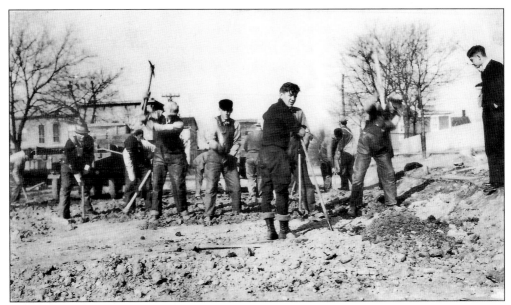

These men use manual labor to accomplish this CWA project on Shenandoah's Second Street in January 1929. Not wanting to miss out on the moment, this unidentified "worker" poses as a matter of record. (Judy Jewell Collection.)

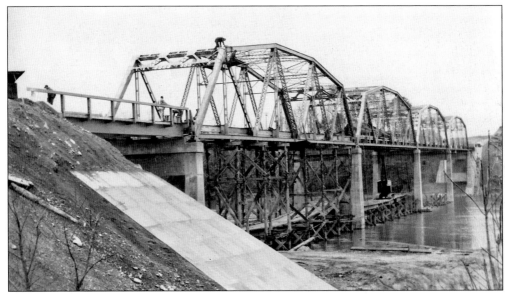

In 1954, T.A. Lovin Company, bridge builders, moved this disassembled Roanoke River bridge from Bugg's Island Dam to Shenandoah, where the structure was re-erected about 50 yards north of the existing bridge. The previous 1890 bridge had been greatly damaged— during the 1896 Flood, an Elkton bridge slammed into and destroyed the east end. (*Page News and Courier* Collection.)

Two

THE INDUSTRIAL PERIOD

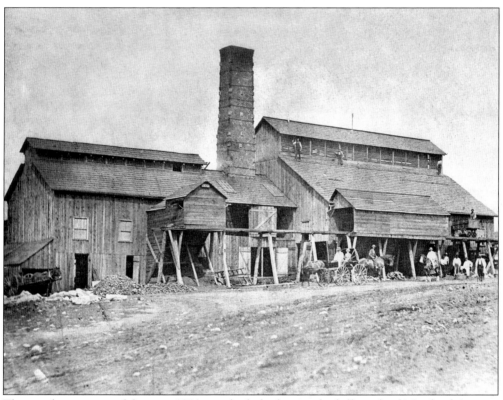

This newly constructed forge, c. 1871, was built further up the hill south of Maryland Avenue after the 1870 Flood destroyed a similar structure. After this disaster, William Milnes Jr., builder of the forge and seen here in white on his horse Dexter, would not seek reelection as a U.S. congressman, resuming operations here instead. He served only a partial term in the 41st Congress because of Virginia's late readmission to the Union on January 26, 1870. (Irvin Judd Jr. Collection.)

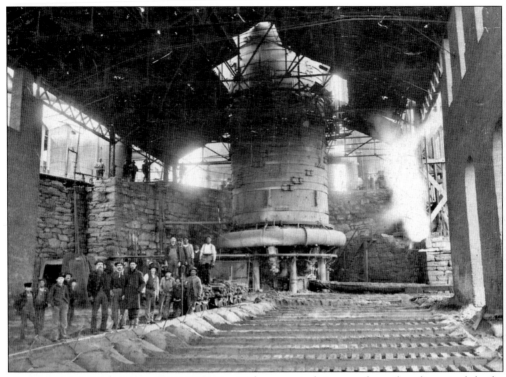

Milnes, capitalizing on the railroad's arrival, built the Big Gem furnace in 1882. His daughter Maggie would light the furnace. Workmen wait inside, where molten pig iron is poured into the grooves on the foundry floor, called "blooms," to make shippable rails of steel. The ore banks were exhausted, and the stack bursting in June 1900 only worsened the company's uncertain economic future. Operations would cease in 1907, and the plant completely dismantled by 1917. (Irvin Judd Jr. Collection.)

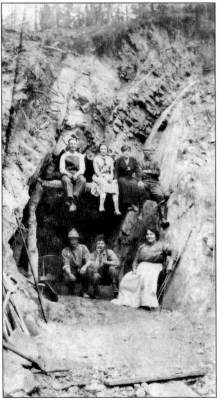

The Compton Mine was opened at a fractured outcrop associated with the Vaughn Summit Fault Zone. Here, locals pose at the mineshaft entrance for this 1910s image. Along with a 300-foot tunnel used to extract the ore in mine cars, an ore wash dam was built in 1921. Worked intermittently by the Compton Manganese Corporation of Pittsburgh since 1916, operations were suspended in the 1950s. (Jimmy Rinker Collection.)

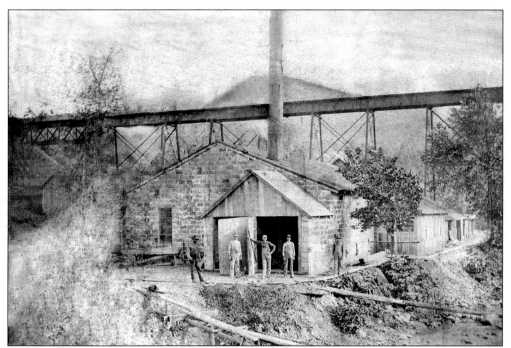

The Oxford Ochre Company of Bentonville, Virginia, their ochre bed being depleted, constructed a plant in Marksville on Honey Run. Superintendent C.B. Foote was in charge of the ochre deposit extractions, which were opened in 1876. In 1898, the N&W raised piers in the midst of the wooden structure, and the new steel bridge was placed in operation without interrupting service. Edgar Kern took this October 10, 1908 photograph showing the operations. (Nancy Painter Collection.)

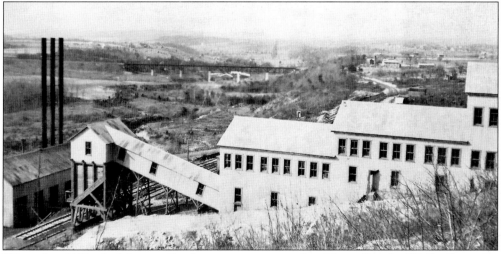

When the old Eureka Mines in Stanleyton were reopened on Honey Run by J.E. Biedler in the 1890s, manganese was in big demand. A one-mile-long narrow-gauge spur was laid by the N&W for shipping the raw ore to Shenandoah's Big Gem furnace, where it was alloyed with steel for strength. The mine was productive for years, but competition caused the need to wane, and it was dismantled in 1939. The Oxford Ochre Mine is in the center background. (*Page News and Courier* Collection.)

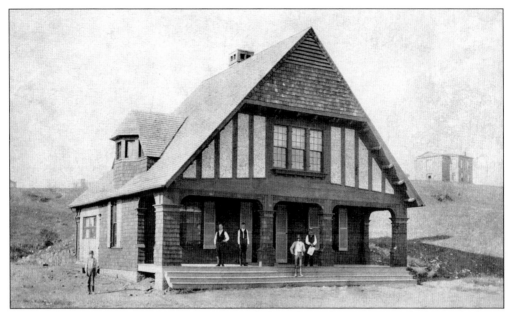

Land and improvement companies were created throughout the country, and Shenandoah was no exception. In continuous operation since 1890, this was the original office of the Shenandoah Land and Improvement Company. Prominent stockholders included Frederick J. Kimball, president of N&W Railroad and William Milnes Jr.'s nephew, and Joseph Sands, general manager of the N&W and original namesake of Sands, Virginia, present-day Stanley. The original Shenandoah School can be seen at far right. (Charles Stevens Collection.)

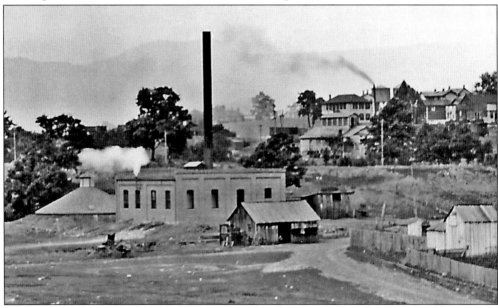

After recovering from the depression of the 1890s, Shenandoah City enjoyed a second growth spurt beginning in 1906, when it installed a then-modern steam-generated electric power plant. J.S. Lauck became superintendent of the new multi-purpose Shenandoah Light and Power Company. Street intersections were lighted with electric arc lamps burning sticks of carbon. (Ed "Casey" Billhimer Collection.)

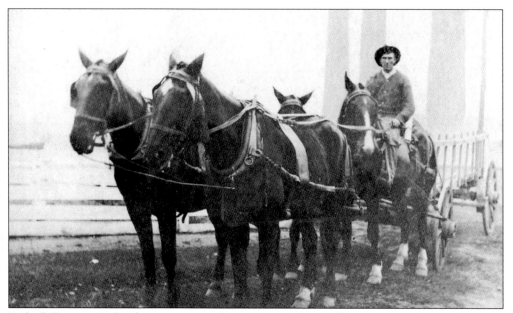

Deford Company's familiar tannery smokestacks are shrouded by a morning fog in this early 1900s photograph, as Solomon "Luther" Printz of Luray drives a four-horse bark wagon. Hundreds brought bark for the tannic acid used in the tanning process. During one especially busy week, over 100 tons were delivered every day, and manager T.S. Brown was a little puzzled as to where to put this necessary commodity. (Gladys Printz Collection.)

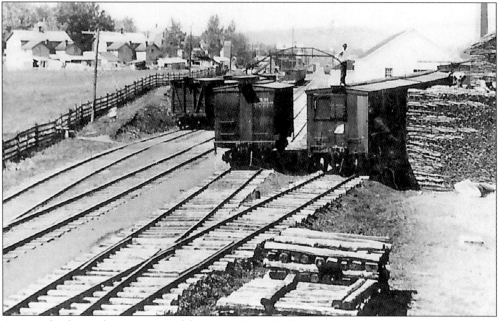

A mutual relationship was created between the Deford Tannery and the Shenandoah Valley Railroad when both came to Luray. Reserves of hand-cut ties lay beside the rail, four tracks wide at this point. In 1892, an arch bridge over the N&W was built, connecting the tannery with their Deford Avenue employees. An unidentified worker waiting on the boxcar catwalk poses unintentionally. (Dan Vaughn Collection.)

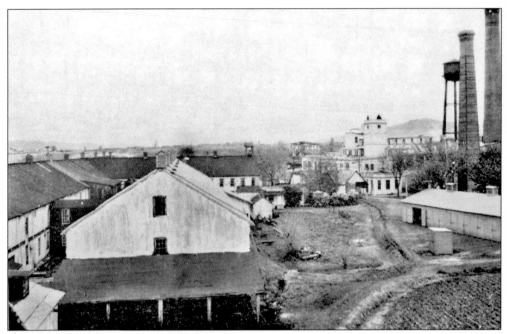

In 1900, Luray Tannery installed a steam electric plant to produce its own electricity. A shipment of leather was sent in April 1893, to display at the Columbian Exposition in Chicago, for Luray leather had already taken first at the 1890 World Exposition in New Orleans. Ochs and Company of Allentown, Pennsylvania, built its first smokestack in 1882, and a 75-foot turntable was constructed just east of the bark barns for turning locomotives. (Dan Vaughn Collection.)

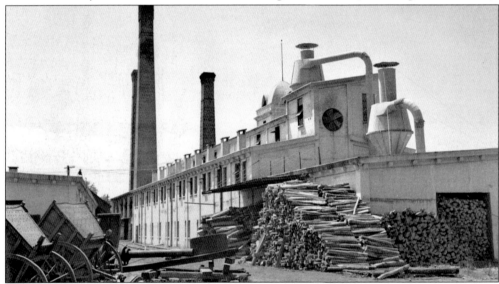

Thomas Deford had initially proposed to erect a tannery in Port Republic, Virginia, but after the farmers in that town resisted this "foreign" industrialist, he chose Luray instead. With construction beginning September 16, 1880, Deford Company tannery had been attracted to Luray by its soon-to-be-completed rail connections and the close proximity to tan bark, used extensively in industrial-scale leather making. Company housing was constructed on nearby Deford Avenue. (*Page News and Courier* Collection.)

At its height of production in the 1970s, the Virginia Oak Tannery processed 1,800 steer hides daily and up to 300,000 pounds of leather a week. Chataigne's 1888–1889 *Business Directory of Page County* listed six tanneries, but none compared to Deford, the largest in the state of Virginia. During construction, the tannery was a scene of activity, with the digging of over 250 vats, each 10 feet deep. (*Page News and Courier* Collection.)

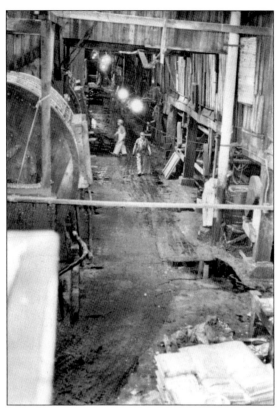

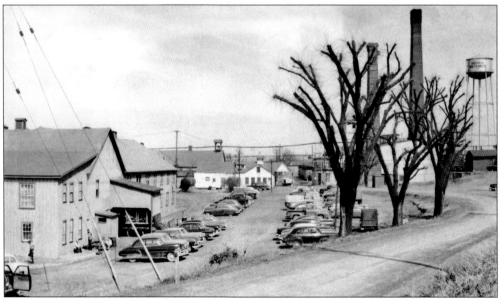

The tannery, which employed up to 250 men, closed for a time in the 1930s. It would be reopened in 1941 as the Virginia Oak Tannery by Arthur Blaut and his son Stephan and remain a Page County industry until it ceased major tanning operations in February 1980, after 100 years. For almost a century, the familiar tannery whistle made contact with all in Luray, employees or not. (*Page News and Courier* Collection.)

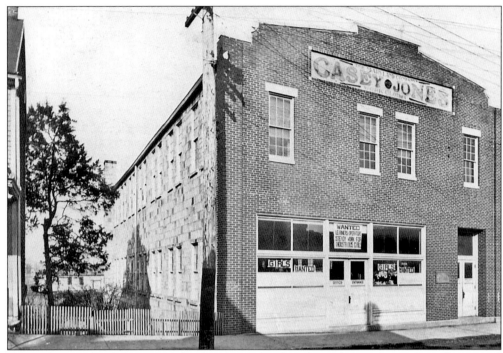

When the Maryland Company of Denton, Maryland, makers of Casey Jones Overalls, opened on West Main Street in 1923, they initiated employment in Luray that has continued to this day. "Wanted, learners—operators, steady work for industrious girls," read the sign on the building's commercially designed front. Andrew Campbell, co-discoverer of Luray Caverns, had earlier lived at this same location. (Ed "Casey" Billhimer Collection.)

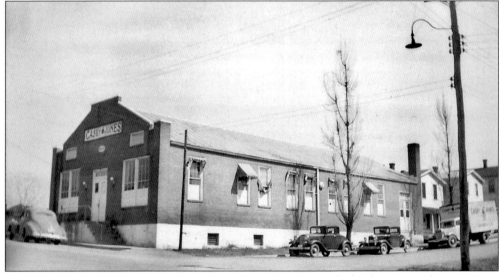

Casey Jones continued its growth in Page when this Shenandoah plant opened in 1925 on Virginia Avenue. Blue Bell Incorporated would later purchase this plant, and the Luray plant as well, in February 1944. Both plants were awarded coveted Army-Navy E Production pennants in recognition of their outstanding service in manufacturing clothing during World War II. (Dan Vaughn Collection.)

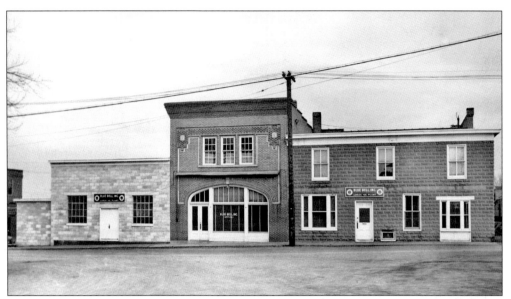

When Casey Jones was bought by Blue Bell in 1944, this overall manufacturer would relocate to Campbell Street and expand operations, including the addition of a cutting room, as seen at left in this photograph. Ashby F. Herndon of Luray, general superintendent of Casey Jones, continued his position here. In 1953, work began on a new 80,000-square-foot warehouse. Growth and a previous fire had initiated the move. (Mrs. Robert L. Herndon Collection.)

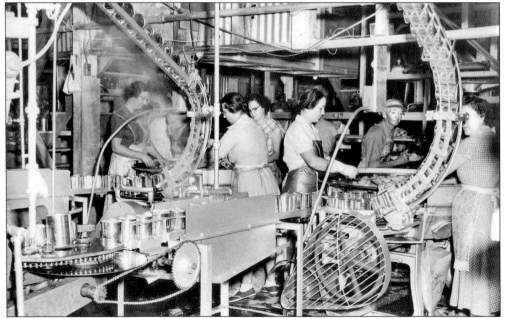

This was a typical day inside the Moyer Brothers canning factory at Stony Man during the summer months, until operations ceased in the late 1960s. Moyer Brothers had begun in 1940, when they purchased the Lucas and Stirewalt factory, built in 1921 by H.F. Lucas and V.P. Stirewalt. With brand names like Page Valley, Stony Man, and Luray Caverns, the cannery canned 500 to 600 cases of peaches daily from the Spitler and Moyer orchards. (*Page News and Courier* Collection.)

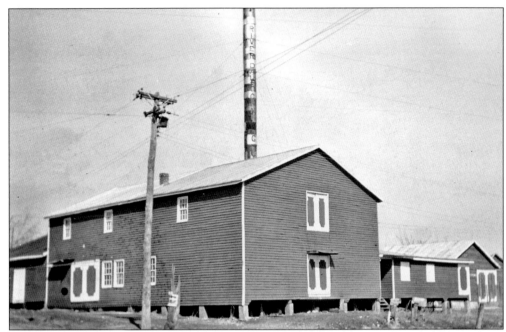

C.D. Price operated the River Dale Canning Company in Alma from the 1930s to the 1950s. There were a number of canneries in Page County at the time, and they employed a large workforce while in the harvest season. River Dale was no exception, with well over 100 employees. (Dan Vaughn Collection.)

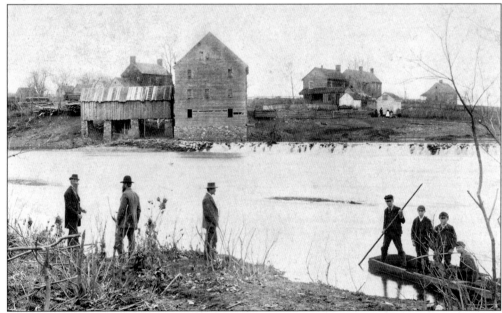

Kauffman's Mill, originally known as Mauck's Mill, was built in 1826 and sold to P.M. Kauffman in 1890. This turbine-powered mill was burned by the Union Army on October 2, 1864, and had barely been rebuilt when destroyed again by the Flood of 1870. Seen in this 1895 photograph from left to right are Enoch V. Kauffman, Philip M. Kauffman, and John Kauffman, with their children in the boat. (Michael Brubaker Collection.)

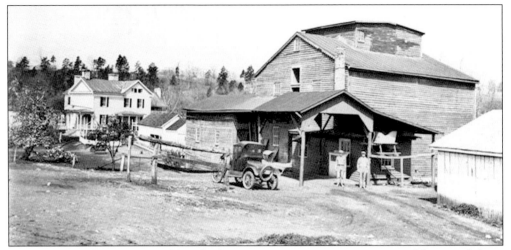

Sandy Hook Mills was operated by Charles W. Carter, one-time postmaster of the now-defunct Willow Bend Post Office. When Carter opened the Luray Mill and Elevator Company in 1895, Frank Brumback, pictured on right, continued mill operations here. An ingenious underground millrace was designed for water to flow through a tunnel, with an underwater turbine powering the mill. Built on a hill safe from floodwaters, the mill burned in 1936. (Jack Cullers Collection.)

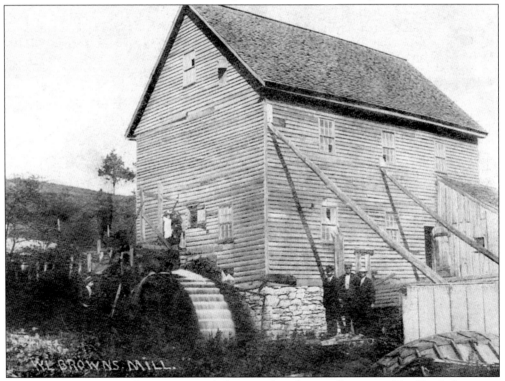

In 1889, E.L. Brown and Sons operated this overshot flour mill, powered by Hite's Spring in East Luray. This was one of 24 merchant flour mills in Page when it formed in 1831. Strangely, the spring sank out of sight just beyond the mill, as if appearing expressly for "Jury" Brown's own benefit. W.L. and Ida Judd Brown continued the mill operations until the mid-1930s, when the Town of Luray purchased the property. (Ricky Clark Collection.)

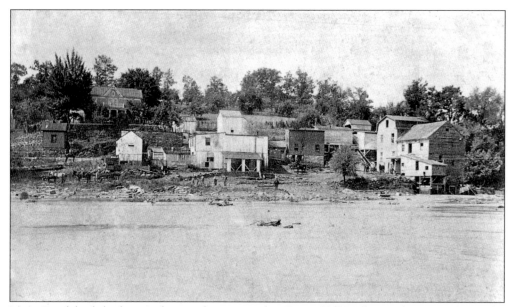

M.A. Roudabush built up a thriving business at his Grove Hill Mill, seen here at right in the 1890s. He had installed water works to every building by 1899, and he even watered his lawn and garden with this system. By 1904, he began operating a ferry to accommodate his customers. Lee Louderback sold farm implements here from 1930 to 1936 before moving to Stanley. The structure burned in 1951. (*Shenandoah: A History of Our Town and Its People.*)

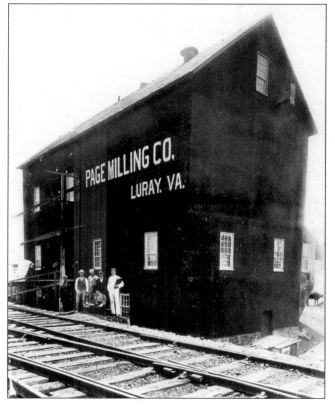

This structure was originally built as the Luray Mill and Elevator Company by C.W. Carter in 1895. E.C. Harnsberger purchased the mill in 1899 and changed its name to Page Milling Company. The Luray Electric Company was established here, with steam power producing electricity to the mill and, in 1904, providing lighting to Luray Caverns. Up until 1920, the mill maintained a cooper shop, building its own barrels. (H. Hudson Price Collection.)

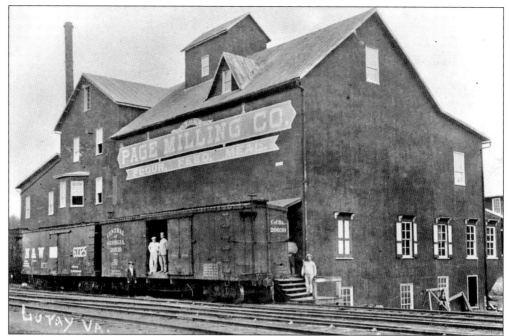

Harnsberger's son, Robert C., joined Page Milling in 1927. Attending flour school in Kansas, he sought out an instant self-rising flour. Robert, experimenting daily using the office staff to critique, perfected his product in 1930; he called it "quick biscuit." The Washburn Crosby Company, later General Mills, offered Page Milling an outright fee of $15,000 for the product. Without wavering, Harnsberger accepted the offer. The name was changed and is now sold by General Mills under the trade name Bisquick. (H. Hudson Price Collection.)

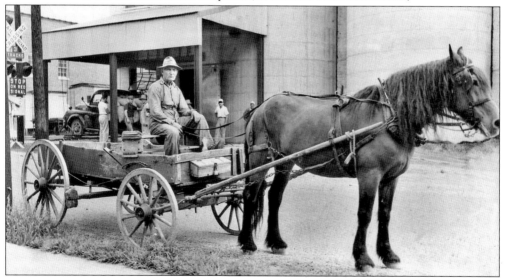

Long lines of large trucks and trailers had formed at Page Milling Company when Alfred Printz of West Luray showed up. After he unloaded his horse-drawn spring wagonload of wheat, he posed for the photographer on July 21, 1955. Page Milling's grain towers were erected in 1948 and added to in 1954 to store bumper crops of wheat from eight surrounding counties. (*Page News and Courier* Collection.)

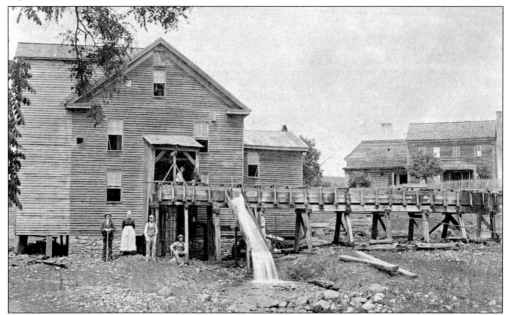

The Verbena Mill was built in 1813 in the community of Waverlie, Rockingham County, Virginia. The sluice spillway operated partially open, possibly for dramatic effect, in this late 1890s photograph. Following the Civil War, Capt. Joseph M. Price, shown at left, inherited the mill. Sadly, it survived the war and two major floods only to be razed in 1936 to widen old Route 12. (*Page News and Courier* Collection.)

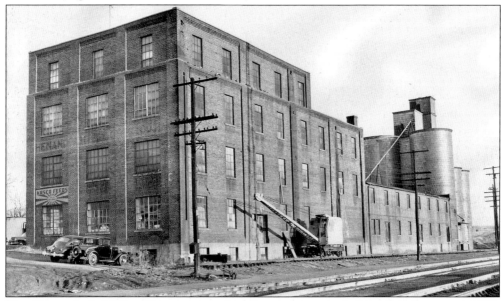

The Shenandoah Milling Company, an initially water-powered gristmill built around 1908, burnt to the ground in the early 1920s. The mill was soon rebuilt by M.A. Roudabush and his son. Producing the Shenandoah, "Stonewall" Jackson, and Robert E. Lee brands of flour, it later changed its name to Shenandoah Flour Mills and sold the Southern Generals label as well. With a government storage program initiated around 1940, the mill's seven grain elevators had a storage capacity of 65,000 bushels. (Irvin Judd Jr. Collection.)

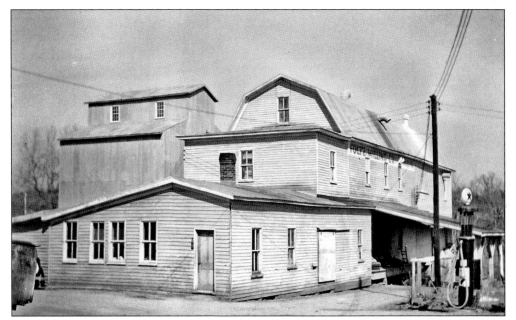

Originally built in 1832, Newport, or Foltz's, was the only mill on the left bank of the Shenandoah River. Owners Elby and Raymond Foltz ran both a sawmill and gristmill at this location and generated electricity that was sold to customers in the Newport area for $1 a month. The mill was destroyed in the floods of 1915 and 1942 and was rebuilt both times, but it discontinued milling in the 1950s. (Dan Vaughn Collection.)

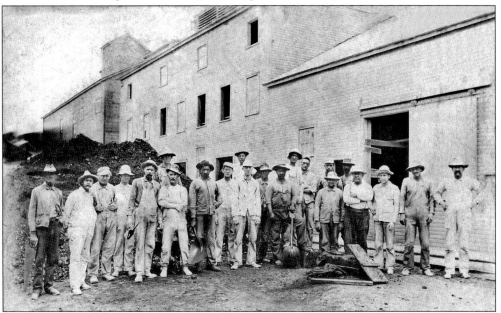

The employees of the original Stanley Milling Company posed here shortly before it burned on May 4, 1909. By now, most mills had converted to steam power to avoid downtime during dry periods. Stanley had no alternative—located next to the N&W, it was not in close proximity to water. Coal is seen here, but wood was the culprit on that destructive day. The mill would be rebuilt. (Town of Stanley Collection.)

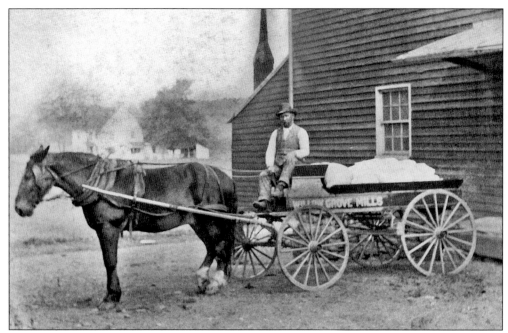

David Henry Gander (father-in-law of Claude R. Grove, owner of Willow Grove Mill) is ready to deliver flour in this photograph taken shortly after Grove purchased the mill in 1900. In 1885, when A.J. Huffman, J.P. Grove, and other associates purchased the mill, it operated as Luray Milling Company. Flour was produced here from 1885 to 1943, with only a short interruption in June 1904, when a new steel overshot water wheel was installed. (Barbara Martin Collection.)

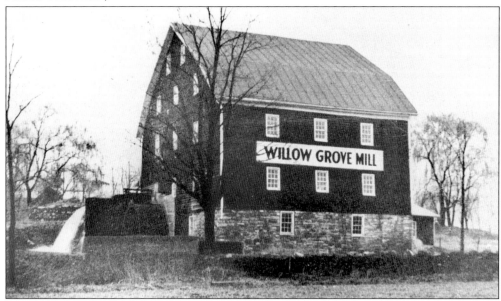

Originally known as Red Mill when built in 1796, Willow Grove Mill is the oldest in Page County. Burned extensively on August 4, 1864, by Sheridan's Federal troops, it was rebuilt in 1867. Powered by an overshot water wheel, Willow Grove has a millpond fed by a millrace from East Hawksbill almost three-quarters of a mile long. (Travis Clark Collection.)

Three

BUSINESS AS USUAL

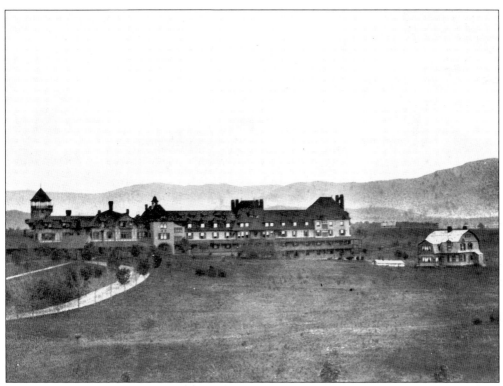

This somewhat eerie view of the old Luray Inn gives a rather stark contrast to its surroundings, with the Blue Ridge Mountains in the distance. The inn cottage on the right was the private dwelling of George Mullin, the proprietor of the inn. A greenhouse, dwarfed in comparison to the overwhelming size of the inn, burned in March 1890, destroying all the plants. (Dan Vaughn Collection.)

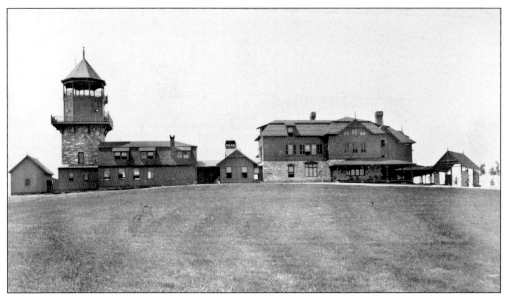

Built by the Luray Cave and Hotel Company, a subsidiary of the Shenandoah Valley Railroad, the Luray Inn is seen here in this uncommon north-side view when it opened on September 1, 1881. The first electricity was generated in Luray just days later on September 19, when current was produced with a dynamo. The "little flame in a glass bottle" created much wonderment. (Virginia Tech Special Collections.)

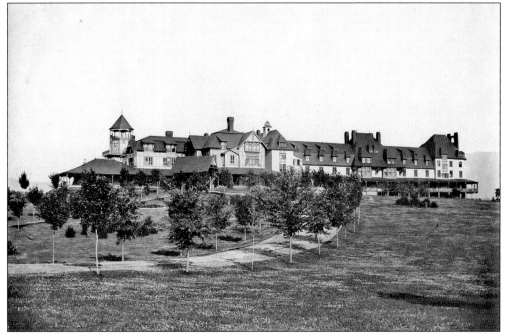

When Philadelphian architect George Pearson designed this extravagant Queen Anne–style inn, contractor Julius Holmes was presented a "spare no expense" rough draft. This enormous structure was fitted with gas lights, telephone, hot water, steam heat, electric bells, a darkroom, and 1,500 feet of porticoes. With a 100-room addition completed in 1883, it became the "Pride of Luray." Little did they know what lay ahead. (*Page News and Courier* Collection.)

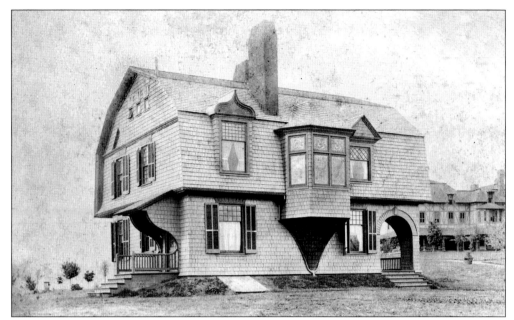

The inn cottage was built in the same quaint manner as the inn itself. The inn captured the rail excursionist's camera lens, so this was a much less photographed structure. Its ornamentation was attractive as well though, with its gambrel truss design, window dormers, bay window, arches, picket railing, and shake shingles. Located some distance from the inn, it was saved from the 1891 fire only to later succumb to an unrelated burning on January 20, 1895. (Warren and Penny Smith Collection.)

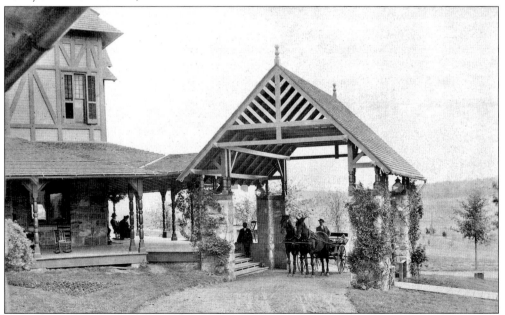

Thousands of visitors to Luray were brought to the *porte cochere*, or carriage door, lit at night by four large gas lamps. Jesse Martin is shown here making the elliptical loop trip from inn to depot and back. After the inn burned, Martin went on to be chief clerk of the Hotel Roanoke and ultimately returned to Luray to become its mayor. (Warren and Penny Smith Collection.)

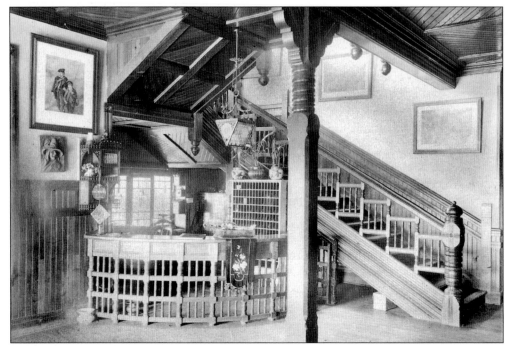

This photograph, from a series taken by prominent Philadelphia photographer William H. Rau in 1883, was commissioned by Rau's business acquaintance William Milnes Jr., president of the Shenandoah Valley Railroad, to promote travel on the newly formed line. One can only wonder of the guests that passed this way. Interestingly though, the extravagance prompted one gentleman to remark that "their party ought to seat the waiters and wait on them." (Warren and Penny Smith Collection.)

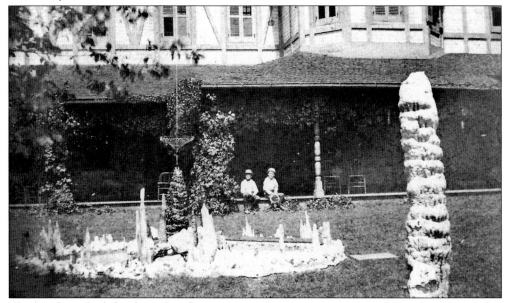

The hotel was built by the railroad more as an advertisement than anything else. Here, laden with stalagmites and stalactites from their own Luray Cave, two unidentified children enjoy this whimsical water fountain on the front lawn. (Warren and Penny Smith Collection.)

The upper portion of the inn tower offered magnificent views from its pavilion observatory. The tower stood for years after the fire, and the Page riflemen used it as a base for target practice. Thereafter, the remaining limestone was crushed to macadamize Main Street. But the greatest irony was that within this 90-foot tower was a 27,000-gallon water tank that stood while the inn burned down around it. (Warren and Penny Smith Collection.)

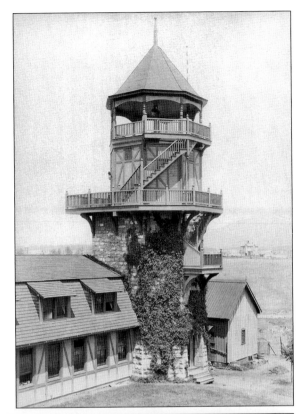

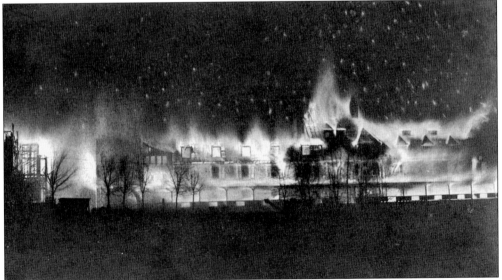

Luray photographer Silas K. Wright captured this fateful image of the Luray Inn in print and later offered copies for sale in his Sunbeam Gallery Studio for 50¢ each. A *Page Courier* advertisement read, "A thrilling scene . . . shows the fire at its greatest height." With a stipulation that the October 5, 1891 auction "continue . . . until completed," the selling had barely finished when the inn burnt to the ground on that November 5, 1891 night. (Dan Vaughn Collection.)

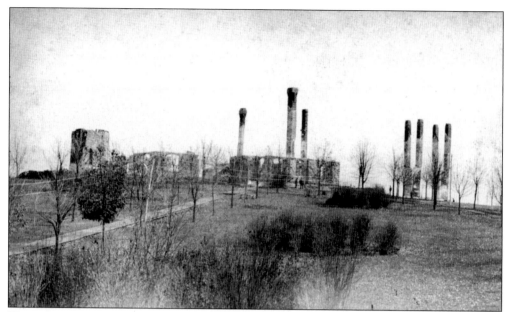

"Disastrous" seems to be the most fitting word for what had happened here. The ruins of the inn looked ghostly on the hill, and although insured for $90,000, it would never be rebuilt. George Mullin would never see the inn's demise, for he died just weeks before in September 1891. The plank walkway now seemed to only intensify the tragedy. Ironically, a plea to join the bucket brigade ran in the *Page Courier*'s November 5, 1891 issue. (*Page News and Courier* Collection.)

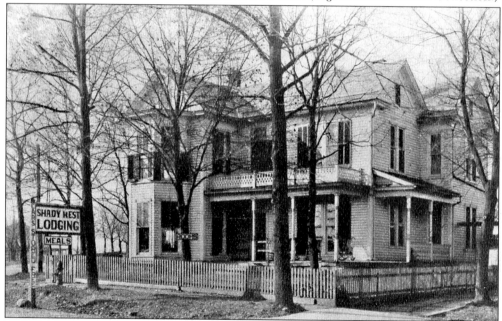

Opposite the Luray Depot, Shady Rest Lodging was ideally located for tourists arriving by rail. In 1928, when this photograph was taken, automobile travel had become fairly popular as well. Shady Rest advertised "cars stored free." With the absence of Luray Inn, tourist homes such as this sprung up throughout Luray. This was a favorite South Broad Street and Virginia Avenue stop operated by Mr. and Mrs. F.H. Tharpe. (*Richmond Times-Dispatch* Collection.)

50

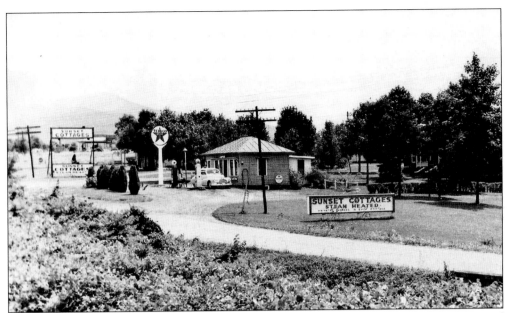

Sunset Cottages, located on U.S. Route 211 east of Luray, was a popular tourist attraction and filling station in the 1930s and 1940s. Proprietor Cletus Presgraves built overnight cottages to accommodate tourists who came with the advent of the automobile. Presgraves sold the cottages in 1947 and purchased the larger Tower Motel, named after the Luray Carillon, on West Main Street. (*Page News and Courier* Collection.)

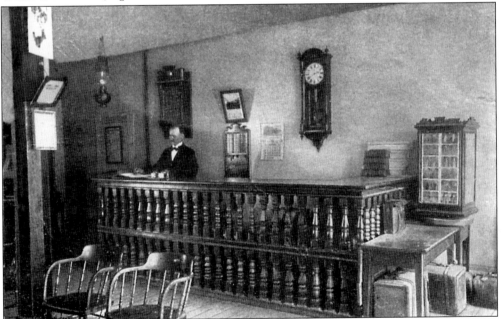

Walter Campbell, owner and proprietor of the Mansion Inn, is seen at the front desk of his establishment in this uncommon 1905 photo. Opened in June 1892, the inn offered year-round lodging, steam heat, electric bells, sanitary plumbing, private baths, good livery, and transportation to the caverns. An 1894 *Page Courier* advertisement read in part, "Furnished in antique oak with hair mattresses and carpet all through. . . ." (Dr. E.W. Gilbert Collection.)

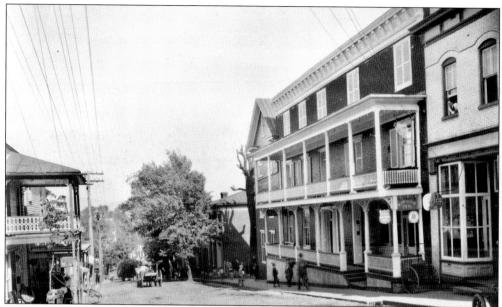

This 1906 West Main Street photograph shows Shandelson's General Merchandise and Frank Jobe's Grocery at left. The Luray Post Office, at far right, would operate here until 1916, when it relocated to the First National Bank Building. Black Russian marble, a hand-carved frieze, and solid mahogany doors were among the interior materials of the Mansion Inn, which operated for over half a century. (Virginia Historical Society Collection.)

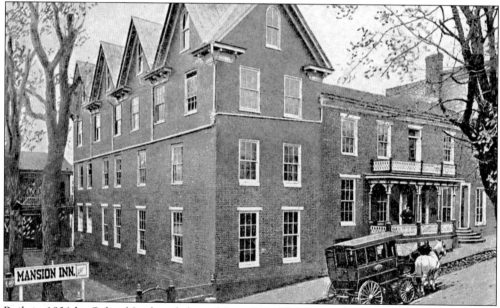

Built in 1831 by Gabriel Jordan, father of Brig. Gen. Thomas Jordan, Page County's only Civil War general. Page County court was held here on July 28, 1831, while the courthouse was under construction. Proprietor Walter Campbell opened the Mansion Inn in June 1892, and the N&W placed the transfer of passengers to the caverns in the care of his Luray Bus Line. After 170 years, the gables were gone when the inn was intentionally burned on November 26, 2003. (Luray Caverns Corporation Collection.)

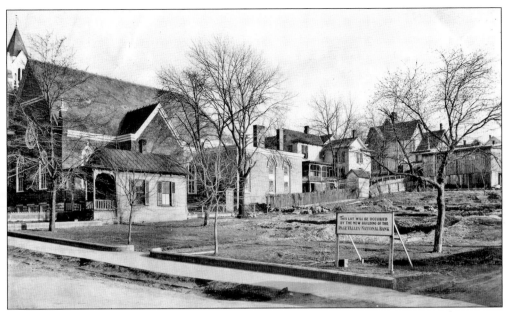

In 1928, this lot was cleared of the antebellum Wade Bohannon House to construct the present Page Valley Bank. The brick Luray Methodist Episcopal Church, at left, would burn three years later and be built back with native limestone. The small building beside the church once housed Wymer's Jewelry Shop, its last tenant before the building was moved in 1969 for a bank addition. (Page Valley Bank Collection.)

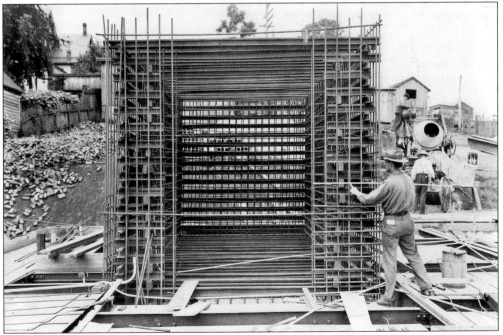

One of the first stages of construction on the new bank had to include its vault. Built of reinforced steel railroad "irons" and concrete mixed on site, the walls were 29 inches thick. The door itself weighed 15 tons and was unloaded at the Luray Freight Depot. (Page Valley Bank Collection.)

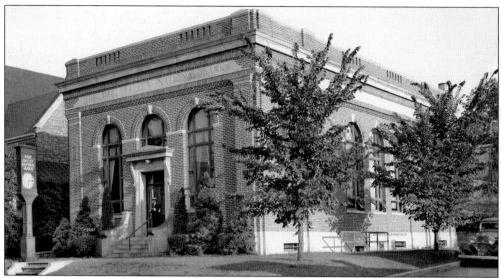

When the private Luray bank of D.F. Kagey and Company failed, leaving Page County without a bank, the Page Valley Bank of Virginia was promptly established, opening its doors on January 3, 1894. They operated in the old Kagey building for nine months, but to rebuild trust, a new bank was built on Bank Street in front of the old structure. Page Valley's third location was impressive. On opening day of May 19, 1928, over 2,500 visitors would come. (*Page News and Courier* Collection.)

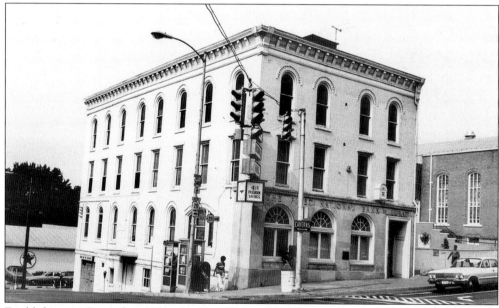

Establishing in December 1901, the First National Bank of Luray initially opened two doors east, for construction would not begin until April 1903. Commonly called the First National Bank, in actuality the building housed numerous activities, including Stover Bros. Grocery, Luray Police Department, Luray Post Office, Roller Furniture, Luray Lending Library, Telephone Exchange, Lafayette Lodge, and others. Mid-1960s improvements of painted bricks and a revolving clock were short lived, being replaced in 1971. (Virginia Department of Historic Resources Collection.)

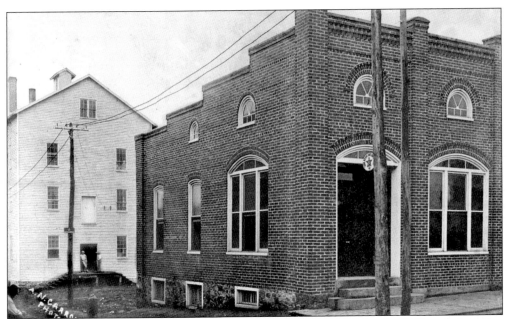

Farmers and Merchants Bank of Stanley was established on December 3, 1909, and their first building was erected on Main Street in 1912. The fire of 1909 was still vivid in the townspeople's memory, so brick buildings were making their way into town. Ironically, the wooden Stanley Milling Company, where that disastrous fire had originated, was again constructed of wood, as seen here. (Pioneer Bank Collection.)

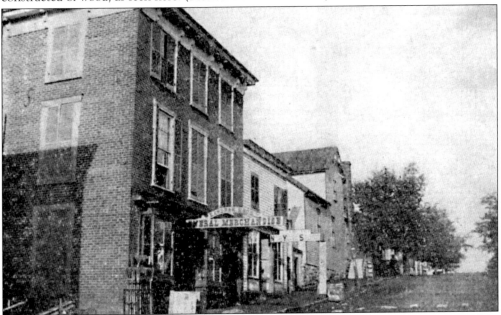

Landram Bros. General Merchandise Store, on West Main Street in Luray, was operated by Charles Landram and his brother Frank when this photograph was taken in 1892. One year later, Charles helped organize the Page Valley Bank. When the citizens of Luray called on the mayor to do something about the "careless and rapid driving," rows of rock were embedded across the street, speed bumps of their day. (Cora Frymyer Collection.)

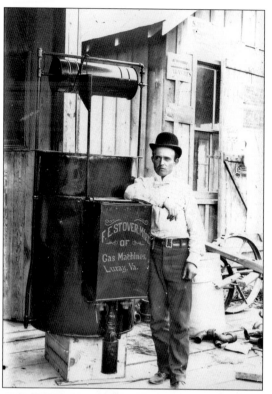

Frank E. Stover, of the Dominion Acetylene Gas Plant, solicited the lighting of Luray with his gas machines. The inventive nature of this entrepreneur prompted G.W. Mead of the Union Carbide Company to highly recommend him for this work in several large towns, but Stover stayed in Luray. Though an improvement over kerosene, the move was ill timed and could not compete with Edison's electric lamp. (*Page News and Courier* Collection.)

C. Edwin Markowitz, seen here in the mid-1950s, operated Center Market on Luray's East Main Street. Interestingly, Markowitz would actually run three Luray grocery stores simultaneously, including East End Grocery and Chapman's Grocery on West Main. His varied merchandise was prominently displayed. (James Earl Kibler Collection.)

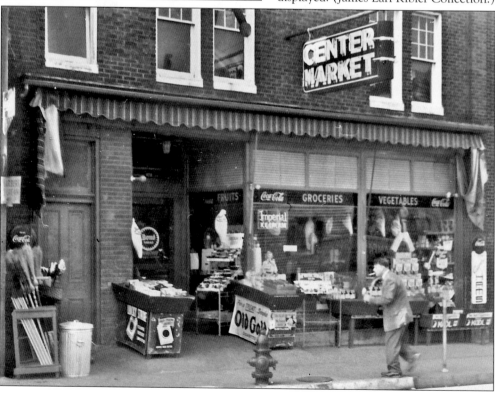

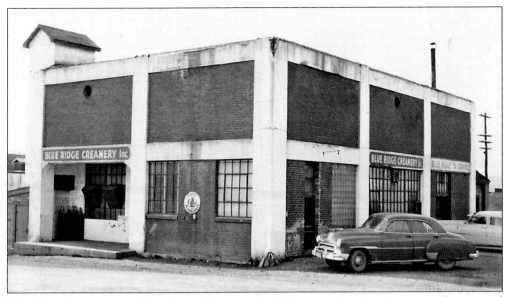

E.C. Harnsberger opened the Luray Creamery in 1919, manufacturing ice cream, butter, and buttermilk. The building was originally built as a cold-storage facility of the Luray Ice Company. When the ice company burned in 1935, the business closed, later reopening as the Blue Ridge Creamery. The Royal Dairy purchased the milk business in 1949. (*Page News and Courier* Collection.)

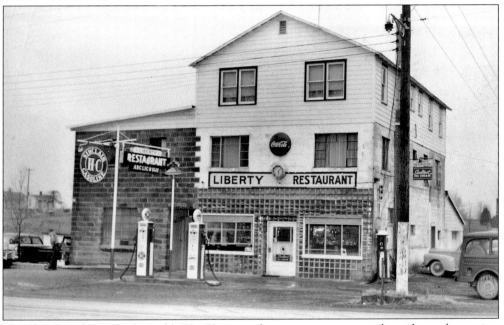

Shortly after the end of World War II, many businesses sprung up throughout the nation sporting patriotic names. One local business was Liberty Restaurant in Shenandoah. Shown in this postwar photograph, it was located at the southernmost town limit, between Trenton and Quincy Avenues. When the photograph was taken, the combination restaurant, convenience store, and filling station sold Sinclair gasoline for 29¢ per gallon. (Ed "Casey" Billhimer Collection.)

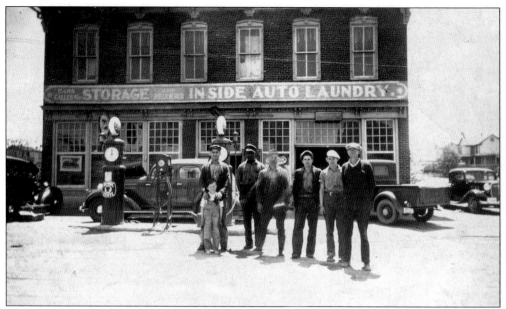

J.W. Batman became a Pontiac dealer in 1937, three years after he started his business. From 1960 to 1964, Rambler automobiles were also sold, and Chrysler-Plymouths were sold from 1964 to 1972. Batman retired in 1970, and his son Dave continued the dealership until 1990. Pictured here, from left to right, are Dave Batman, J.W. Batman, John D. Williams, Lewis Beaghan, Harold Morris, Buddy Orye, and John Good. (Dave Batman Collection.)

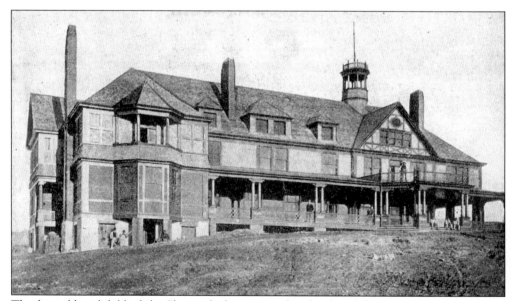

The framed hotel dubbed the Shenandoah was completed in late fall of 1890. Occupying a site at the end of Shenandoah Avenue, it would succumb to the same fate as the Luray Inn when fire consumed it on March 19, 1891. A third railroad-owned hotel at Stony Man would also burn, all three in less than a year. Although rebuilt, the resort hotel it was meant to be never materialized, and the hotel was later razed. (Dan Vaughn Collection.)

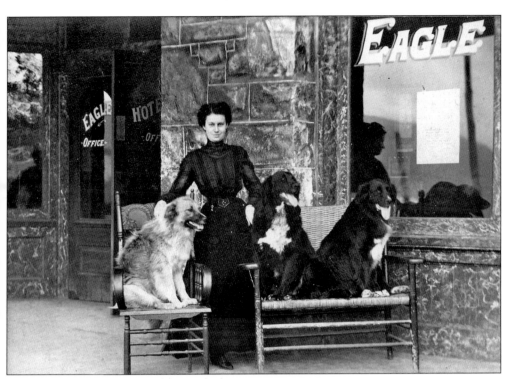

George Harris's daughter, Mable, no doubt worked at the front desk of the Eagle Hotel, and shown here with the greeters of the day, she was a welcome sight to trainloads of Norfolk and Western excursionists arriving in town. Unfortunately, the sign in the window is actually a flyer advertising the sale of the hotel at an auction to take place on May 25, 1937. (Karen Miller Collection.)

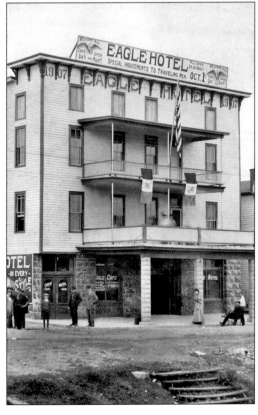

The Eagle Hotel opened on October 1, 1907, with proprietor George Harris touting a day-and-night dining café and 30 rooms for overnight accommodations. Located on Shenandoah's First Street across from the depot, it was first choice for many of N&W's rail passengers. A traveling painter, not being able to pay, was allowed to paint murals on the interior. Although the hotel has been closed since 1937, a mural featuring an entire N&W train still remains. (Charles Stevens Collection.)

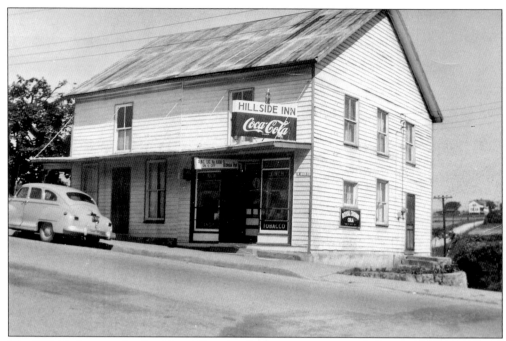

The Hillside Inn, run by David and Beatrice Redman, was previously known as Izzy's Inn. An advertising card read, "When Visiting the Shenandoah Valley, Stop at the Hillside Inn, Delicious Food, Box Lunches and Ice Cold Drinks." This combination restaurant and inn operated on Luray's West Main Street. (Roxcella J. Brown Collection.)

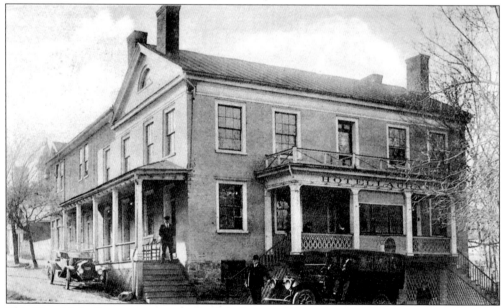

This West Main Street structure was built by Emanuel Grove in the 1830s. Living here, he also ran a mercantile store facing South Court Street until 1856. In 1883, Joseph Parkinson converted the building into a hotel, which he aptly named "Hotel Laurance," after his wife Laura. In 1902, H.B. Mims purchased the building, and his family continued the business until they opened the Mimslyn Inn. (Lyn Good Collection.)

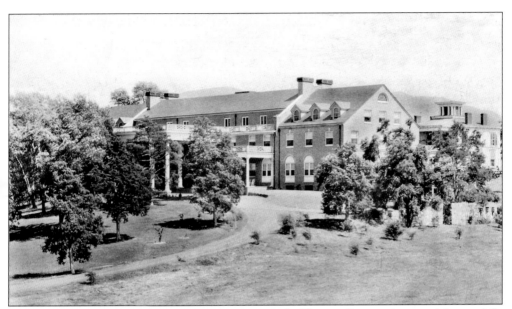

The Mimslyn Inn opened in May 1931. First Lady Eleanor Roosevelt stayed here while President Franklin D. Roosevelt launched the Civilian Conservation Corps (CCC) at Shenandoah National Park. The Mimslyn Inn was designed by local architect J. Raymond Mims for his brothers, Ralph and John W. Mims. The family had previously operated the Mansion Inn and Hotel Laurance. The Borst Mansion, at far right, was moved for construction, dismantled, and reconstructed piece-by-piece on Court Street. (*Page News and Courier* Collection.)

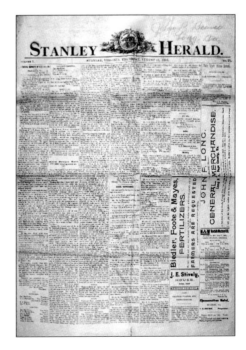

Rev. T.S. Dalton, proprietor and editor of the *Stanley Herald*, began printing this local newspaper in 1891. It was a very informative paper that kept abreast of the Stanley news and had the blessing of Luray's *Page Courier*, but with the railroad's bust and the depression of the 1890s, the *Herald* was suspended in 1898. This particular issue was hand-addressed to John P. Beaver of Long, Page County. Note advertisements on the front page. (Gloria Biller Messerley Collection.)

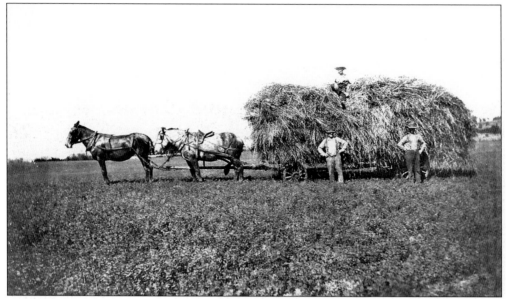

"A thing of the past" best describes this early 1920s scene of a three-horse team pulling a wooden-spoke hay wagon on J. Gil Grove's Fairview Farm south of Luray. With the advent of mechanized farm equipment, production increased and the burden of labor was lessened, but workhorses and a way of life passed. (Ann Vaughn Collection.)

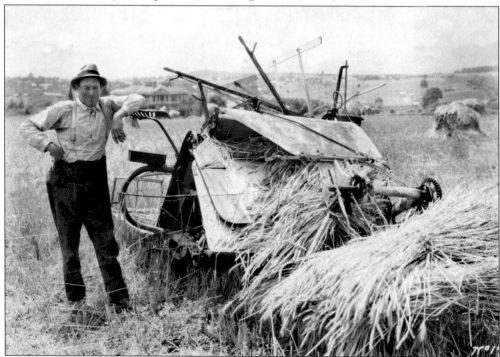

Here, near Yager's Spring north of Luray, is John Ponn with his horse-drawn binder, harvesting barley. Grain shocks were a common sight in the surrounding Page County countryside. The farmer was kept busy while operating all the levers on this very familiar piece of equipment of the day. (Steward Yowell Collection.)

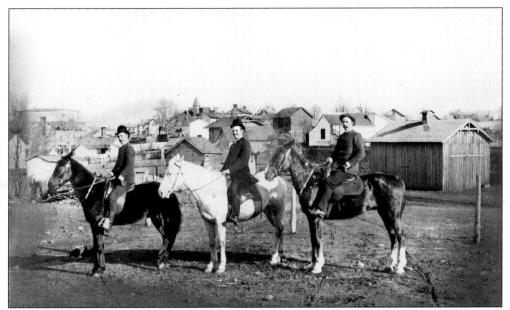

These Luray businessmen posed for this photograph around 1885 at Long's Stable in Luray's East End. The newly laid Shenandoah Valley Railroad and its stock pens can be seen behind the gentleman on the right, and behind the central rider's derby is the railroad's freight station. Other recognizable structures include the turret of a Main Street home, St. Mark's Lutheran Church's steeple, and the Deford Company tannery on the left. (*Page News and Courier* Collection.)

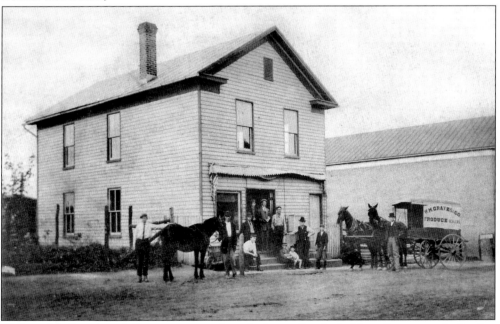

William M. Graves and Company, a produce dealer on Stanley's Main Street, was built after the devastating fire of 1909. Mr. Graves made horse-and-wagon deliveries to other local stores at the time this photo was taken around 1915. The store was later operated as a grocery business and was simply known as the Country Store. (Dan Vaughn Collection.)

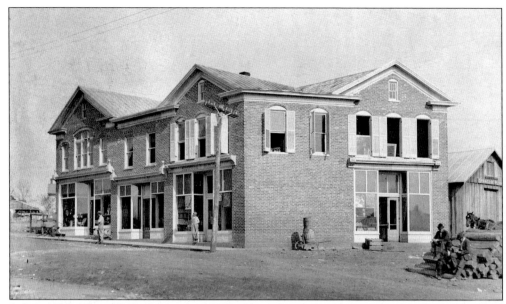

Lake's 1885 *Atlas of Page County* lists T.W. Shryock as a "Dealer in Dry Goods, Notions and General Merchandise, Store at Sands, P.O.," of which he was once postmaster. Two disastrous fires in Stanley in less than 15 years would force Shryock to finally rebuild his storehouse in brick, as seen here around 1915. The Stanley Post Office later occupied the bottom center portion of this building. (Town of Stanley Collection.)

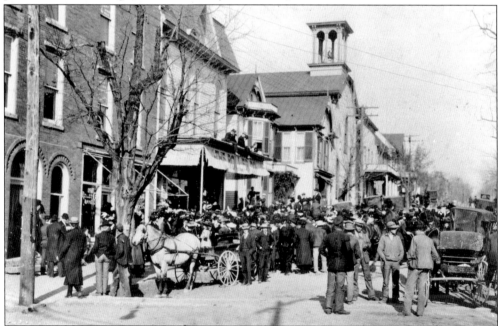

This fascinating photograph of "Roller Day," at the Roller Company on East Main Street in Luray, shows a multitude of patrons who came to town every September for this annual event. By 1906, they had opened their annex in the First National Bank Building, built just three years before. In 1924, Luray Baptist Church was slated for replacement and a name change to Main Street Baptist. (Virginia Historical Society Collection.)

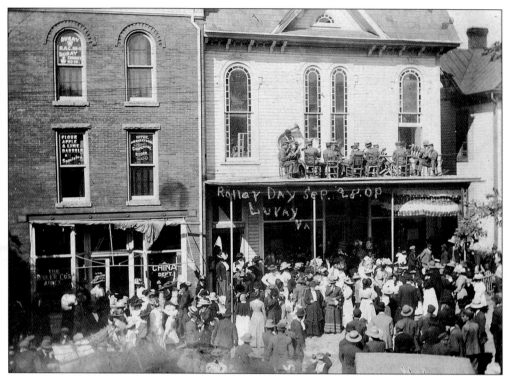

Local photographer Dan F. Holmes would capture another view of the activity that was present at the Roller Company's Roller Day on September 28, 1909. A local band, probably the Luray Cornet Band, found a free space to perform as they continue playing at midday. A 1911 calendar card advertised furniture, pianos, organs, and everything for the home. (Ann Vaughn Collection.)

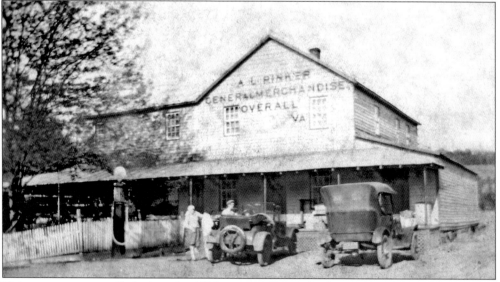

This structure, originally built in the 1890s as a warehouse for the F.H. Borden Barrel and Stave Factory in Overall, is still standing. Arthur L. Rinker would later operate his general merchandise store here, as well as the Overall Post Office. The September 22, 1864 Battle of Milford, a former name for the community, was fought here. (Jimmy Rinker Collection.)

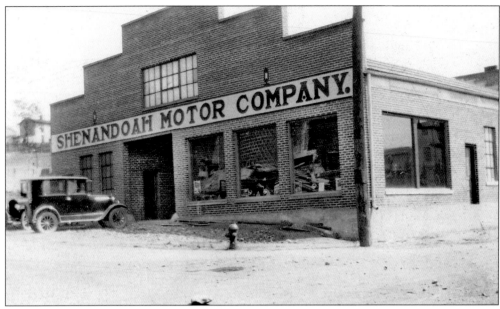

Ray Huffman, mayor of Stanley, and his brother Clark ran the Shenandoah Motor Company, an authorized Ford dealer located at the corner of First Street and Maryland Avenue. In 1925, the building would unfortunately be destroyed in a fire but was rebuilt, and E.E. Haines continued the dealership. A livery stable had previously operated on the site. (Dan Vaughn Collection.)

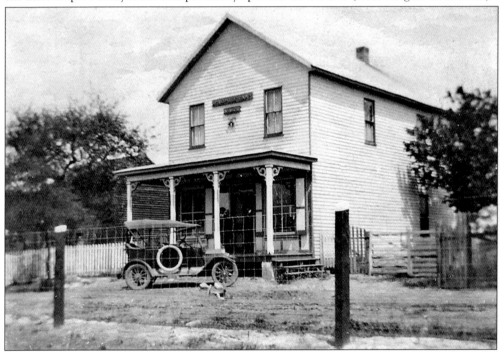

Brothers Ralph O. and K.T. Rothgeb opened for business in this two-story frame store in Leaksville in 1920, but the building itself probably dates to about 1900. This general merchandise store sold staples like candy, dry goods, and clothing, as well as luxuries like oysters, until its closure in 1958. (Dorothy Rothgeb Collection.)

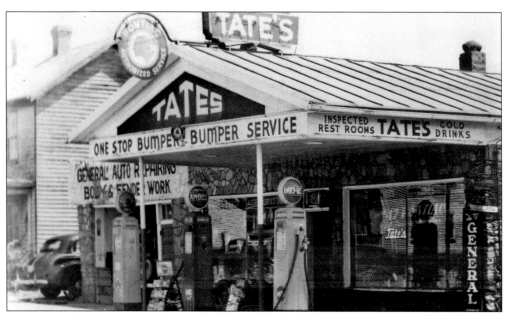

Around 1937, Manly Tate of Luray purchased this East Main Street Pontiac dealership from Bergie Judd, who had established the franchise. GM trucks were sold here shortly after this picture was taken in 1947. During World War II, no cars were sold because of rationing. Tate acquired a long list of buyers during that time. After the dealership ended in 1955, used vehicles were sold here until 1960. (Doc Bosley Collection.)

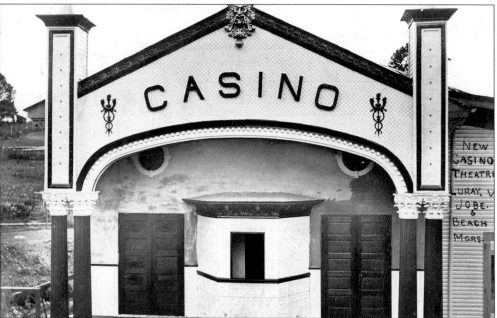

When John R. Jobe opened the Casino Theater in 1911, it became Luray's first moving picture house. An advertisement in a 1912 publication called it "Luray's popular boardwalk attraction," referring to the wooden walkways that lined Main Street at the time. Located on the southwest corner of the Hawksbill Bridge on West Main Street, the building burned down on November 1, 1929. (*Page News and Courier* Collection.)

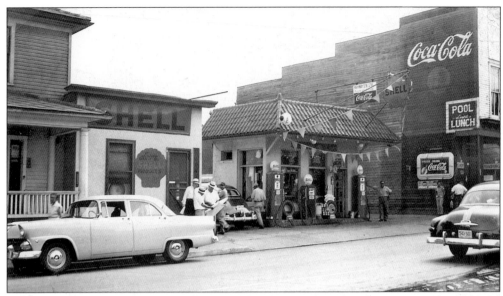

Owners Harry Zepp and A.E. "Squire" Hackley discuss plans for the construction of a new Parkway Shell Gas Station on East Main Street with a Shell Oil representative. Leaning against the gas pumps is Charlie Shenk, a delivery driver for the station. The office of Luray Gas and Oil is a renovated portion of the old Dr. Frank Grove house on left. Leo Strickler Sr. operated a billiard parlor on right. (Eileen Sours Collection.)

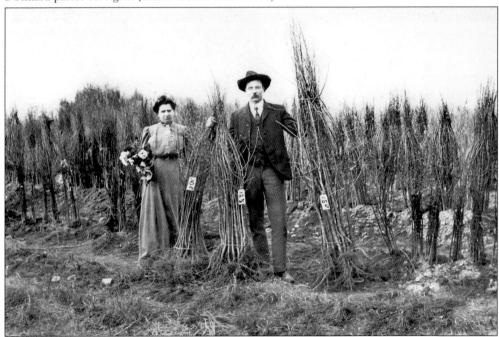

This glass-plate image by the Frensley Studio of Luray shows Arvilla and Albert Bolen with fruit trees shipped by train to the Elgin Depot in Kimball. In an 1894 issue of *Page News*, he advertised his Page Valley Nurseries as having "250,000 fruit trees and ornamental trees of all kinds for sale." One such apple variety sold in 1899 was "Kimball." Bolen operated the nursery from 1898 to 1931. (*Page News and Courier* Collection.)

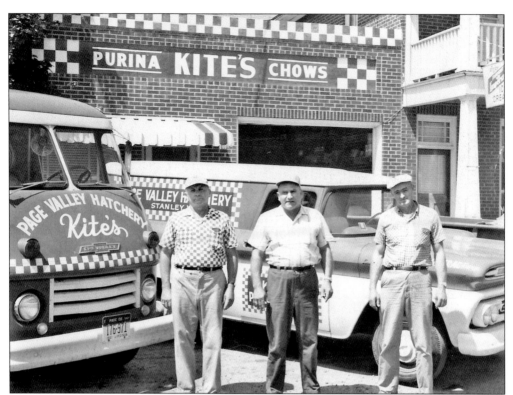

The poultry industry in Page was growing at an ever-increasing pace, and Kite's Page Valley Hatchery at Newport had increased their numbers to keep free-range growers satisfied. Multiple grain towers had been erected at Stanley's N&W depot, allowing them to receive rail shipments for the large amounts of feed needed daily. Seen here in 1961 are, from left to right, Gilbert Housden, owner Wilson Kite, and Pete Price. (Bill and Sylvia Deavers Collection.)

Wilson Kite's father, Howard W. "Harry" Kite, initially started the business and had expanded his Newport operation north. With the incorporation of rail delivery, these grain towers would become a convenient annex for Wilson Kite to deliver to the growers in Stanley when he took over the operations. (Bill and Sylvia Deavers Collection.)

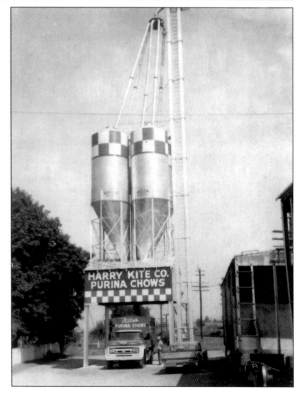

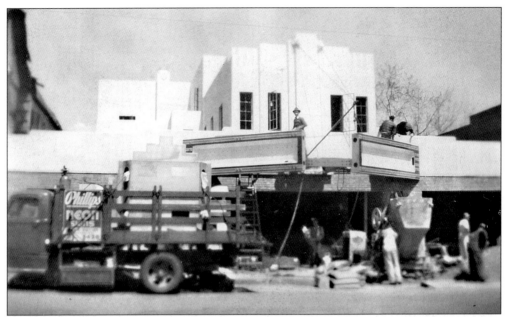

When the Page Theater Corporation announced the construction of a second theater in Luray, the old movie house became referred to as the "Bridge Theater." D.F. Aleshire, manager of the Bridge Theater, would oversee the operations at this location as well. A well drilled 867 feet deep was used in the elaborate air conditioning system. (Lloyd Kibler Collection.)

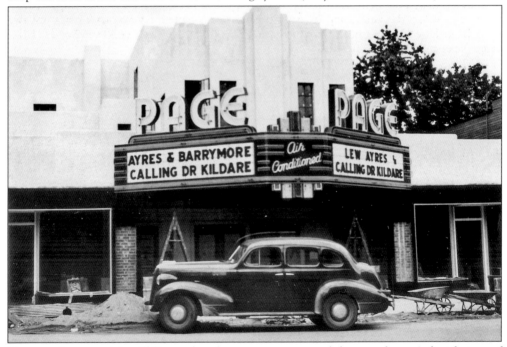

Construction materials still lingered as the marquee presented the new theater's first feature of *Calling Dr. Kildare*, starring Lew Ayres and Lionel Barrymore. This modern state-of-the-art structure, opened in May 1939, had seating for 1,000. Admission was 15¢ for children and 30¢ for adults, 5¢ more than the Bridge Theater. (Dan Vaughn Collection.)

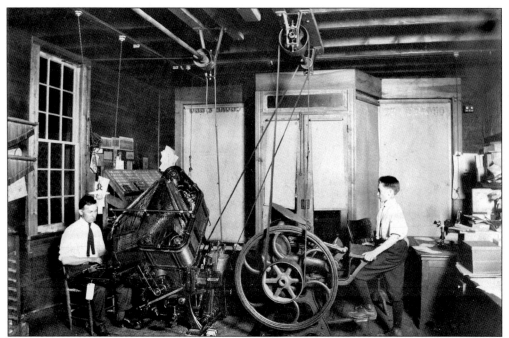

Page News's Orville H. Aylor, at left with linotype, and Carroll E. Beach, at press, are in the Grove and Bro. Store in this 1908 photo. In 1890, *Page News* was bought, the name changed to *Luray Times*, and the paper was printed daily by the Valley Land and Improvement Company. When the land company went bankrupt, a complete reversal took place just two years later. *Page Courier* once printed a six-page book-sized edition on November 25, 1911. (*Page News and Courier* Collection.)

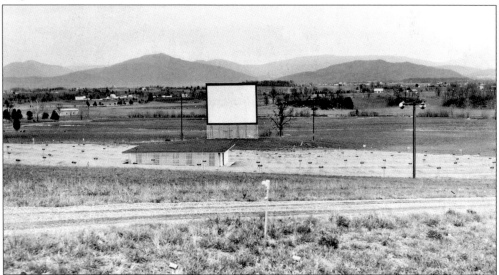

In September 1951, the Page Theater Corporation announced plans to buy seven acres of land and construct a drive-in theater in the Luray area. The new drive-in was built about two miles south of the town and opened in the summer of 1952. With a capacity of 226 automobiles, the theater charged an admission price of $1 each, regardless of the occupancy. (*Page News and Courier* Collection.)

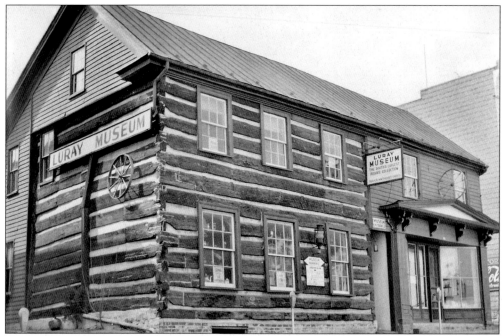

The Luray Museum contained a formidable collection of rarities amassed by owner L. Ferdinand Zirkel's mother, Mollie, when it opened in May 1938. On the very day Page County was formed in 1831, its first baby was born in this building. The museum closed in 1960, and the contents were dispersed in an auction that lasted for days. The log structure was dismantled and incorporated into a house in the Strole Farm area. (*Page News and Courier* Collection.)

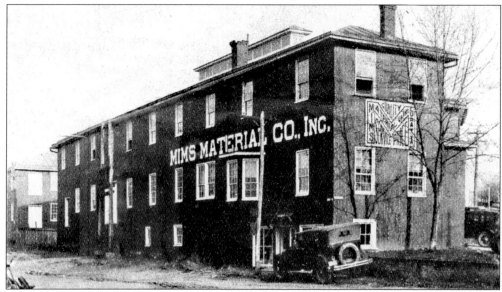

A War Department contract to produce 4,100 trestles was awarded to the Mims Material Company, shown here in 1928. Page County's first television demonstration took place here in February 1948, when a representative of the General Electric Company was on hand to conduct the presentation. Lowell Baughan, later purchasing the business in 1950, renamed it Baughan Construction Company. (*Richmond Times-Dispatch* Collection.)

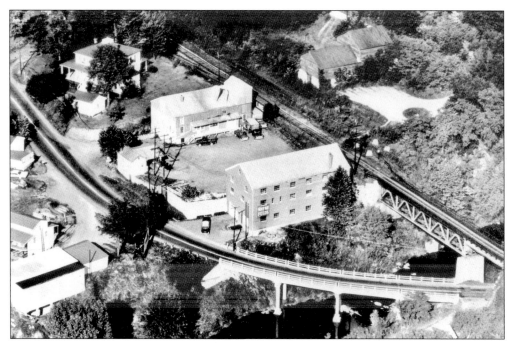

Farmers seeking a way to save on costs organized the Page Cooperative Farm Bureau on August 24, 1921, with Nelson H. Clark as its first president, thus making it the oldest in the state. This October 1962 aerial shot shows the operations of the day. It would be three years before the construction of the new grinding mills. Growth necessitated the three-story brick building in 1949, replacing a primitive warehouse at the same site. (Page Cooperative Farm Bureau Collection.)

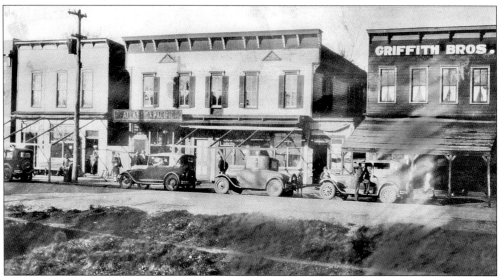

Seventy years after the 1859 establishment of the Great Atlantic and Pacific Tea Company (A&P), this Shenandoah location on First Street was photographed on April 22, 1929. Seen in this image, from left to right, are J.A. Orye's Barber Shop, A&P, Hisey Bros. Pharmacy, a 12-foot-wide newsstand with current newspapers "wallpapering" the building's front, and Griffith Bros. (Russell Comer Collection.)

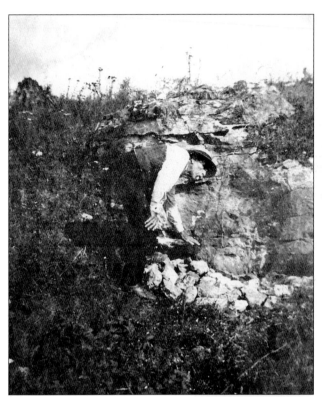

New York Herald correspondent Maj. Alexander Brand Jr. inadvertently named the cave in an article titled "The Luray Caverns." Benton Stebbins had planned to call it "the Beauty of the World," but the October 19, 1878 *Herald* story took precedence. Stebbins, who took this staged photograph of Andrew Campbell at the discovery site, was elected mayor of Luray on March 10, 1881, but his elation would be short-lived—six weeks later, a court reversal on the caverns' ownership was devastating. (*Page News and Courier* Collection.)

With floors and halls lit by 1,000 candles, 200 viewed the caverns on its November 6, 1878, "Day of Illumination," collecting $91 on this first official tour. A.W. McKim Drug Store would later sell magnesium ribbon for visitors to better see the "wonder." Benton Stebbins allowed stalactites to be exhibited in a Tiffany and Co. window, leading to a major article in the *New York Times*. (Dan Vaughn Collection.)

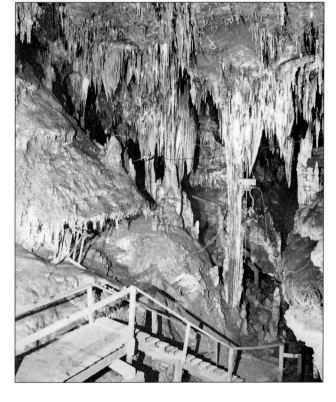

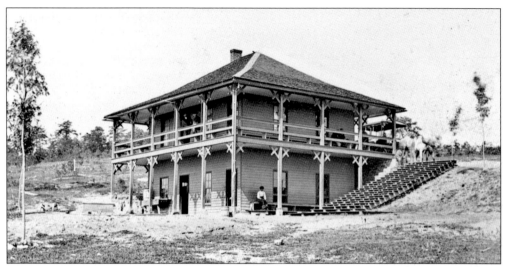

A hack unloads tourists at the Luray Caverns entry house, built shortly after the caverns' discovery. Tin reflectors used in exploring the cave were made in Andy Campbell's tinsmith shop. The reflectors affected the explorers' compass, distorting the mapping accuracy. Andrew Campbell, the first person to enter the caverns, with his nephew Quint Campbell following behind, remarked firmly to the younger lad, "Don't you say anything about this, do you hear?" Those words later proved he purchased the property under false pretenses. (Virginia Tech Special Collections.)

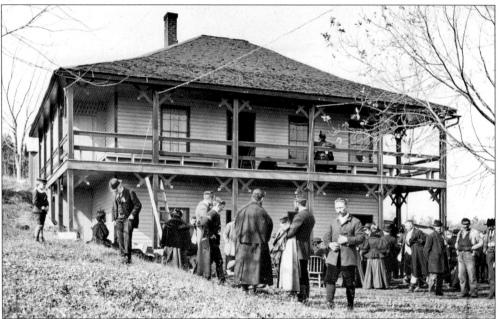

When this rare glass plate image was taken by Philadelphia photographer Charles Pancoast in November 1895, the Luray Caverns had only been discovered 17 years earlier. This original entrance house to the cave had porticoes on all sides, and within, visitors would register, pay admission, and be assigned a guide. Caverns guides, co-discoverer Andrew Campbell among them purportedly unbuttoning his coat, are between tours outfitted in heavy coats, boots, and hats, rugged wear for their subterranean employment. (George Eastman House Collection.)

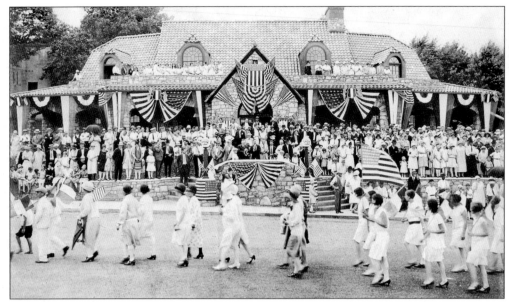

The dedication of this new entrance building in August 1928 coincided with the 50th anniversary of the discovery of the caverns. A bronze plaque honoring Page County's World War I battle dead was also dedicated and put on permanent display within the cave. Built of native sandstone from Massanutten Mountain, the building was designed by J. Raymond Mims, architect of both the Luray Singing Tower and the Mimslyn Inn. (*Page News and Courier* Collection.)

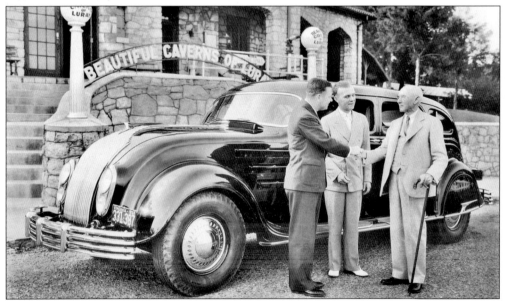

This 1934 Chrysler Airflow Imperial was a gift to Col. Theodore Clay Northcott, founder of the Luray Caverns Corporation. Colonel Northcott, originally renting the property, purchased the caverns from the railroad in 1905, thus initiating a family business spanning four generations. During the Great Depression, there were few travelers, so to supplement these lean years, he began a mushroom operation in the old Ruffner Cave nearby. (Luray Caverns Corporation Collection.)

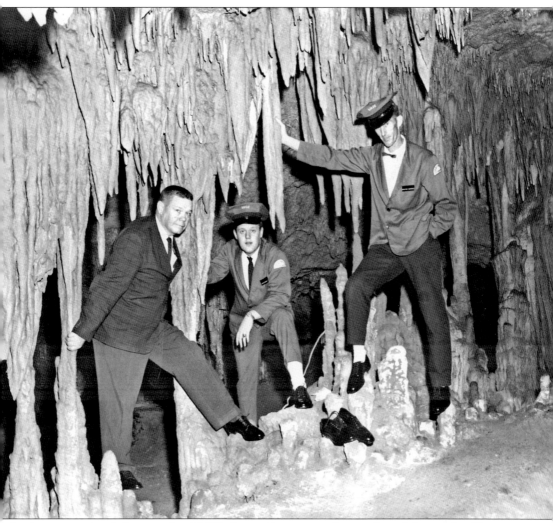

In this promotional photograph of 1955, Luray Caverns employees, from left to right, Kenny Campbell, Wayne Bradley, and Grafton Campbell pose with shoes made with Virginia Oak Tannery leather. Even though the tannery has ceased operations, the caverns continue on after more than 125 years. T.J. Berry once wrote in the old *Page Courier*, "Every town should have a cave, no town is complete without one." (Luray Caverns Corporation Collection.)

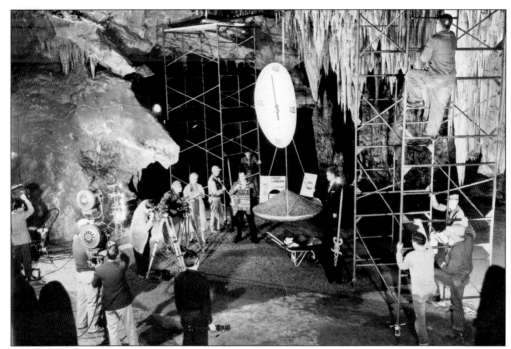

The caverns have always maintained a close relationship with the community. This promotional photograph, taken in 1958, shows the enormous amount of coins donated; this time to the American Cancer Society. Since the inception of the Wishing Well in 1954, nearly half a million dollars has been given to various charities. (Luray Caverns Corporation Collection.)

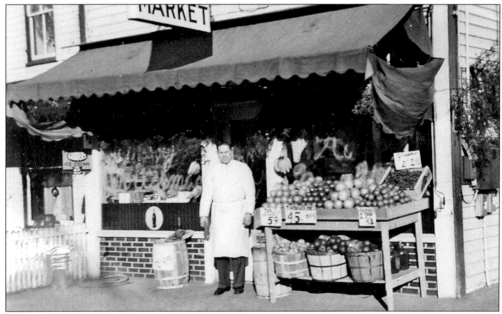

Opened on November 21, 1947, by Mrs. Iva Anderson, this popular East Main Street market carried a complete line of groceries. After World War II, there was a need for markets such as this, and with a prime location, it was very successful until it closed in the 1970s. Shown is Iva's husband, Garland Anderson. (Iva Anderson Collection.)

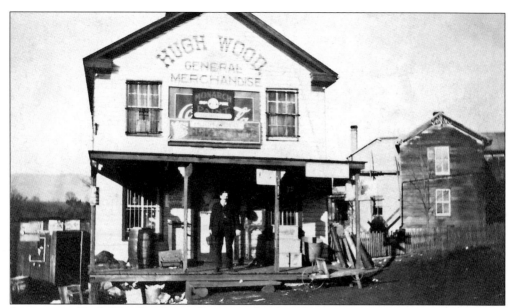

Store owner Hugh Wood took a mid-morning break and posed for this early 1920s photograph on Rileyville's Main Street. His goods were all displayed for the day, with an old wheelbarrow, at right, used extensively over the years for carting merchandise from the adjacent Rileyville Depot to customers' wagons and, later, their automobiles. (Nora Belle Comer Collection.)

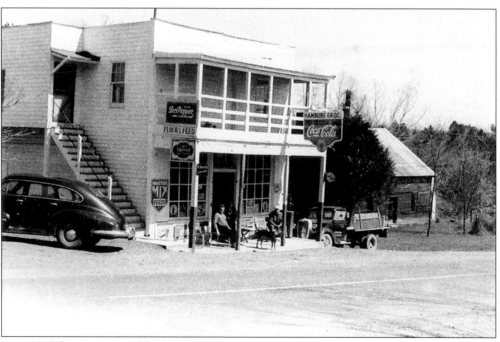

In 1898, Thompson Strickler built a one-story storehouse in Hamburg that his son Benton operated. Benton was the only postmaster of the one-time Eura, Virginia Post Office that operated within the store from 1899 to 1905, named after his sister, Eura (Strickler) Judd. By the time of this 1948 photograph, a second story had been added. Harvey J. Earnhart, operator at the time, ran the store until it closed in late 1958. (Dan Vaughn Collection.)

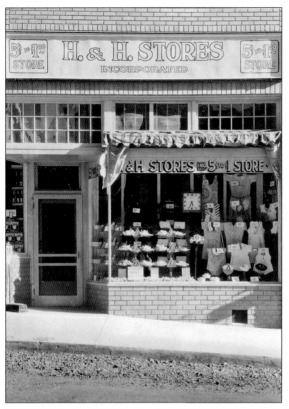

C.P. Harrell, a manager for the F.W. Woolworth Co., while passing through Luray in the late 1920s, noticed it did not have a variety store. So he, along with partner L.R. Hudson, established Harrell and Hudson Variety Store on Main Street in November 1931. By January 1946, Harrell had bought out Hudson's interest, and C.P.'s son, Philip Harrell, along with his family, continued to operate H&H in Luray until it closed its doors on January 8, 2000. (Curtis and Philip Harrell Collection.)

F.W. Berry built this popular hardware store in 1883, and although his stock seemed to be arranged in absolute confusion, he could locate any article you desired on a moment's notice. The horse and dog in this 1888 S.K. Wright photograph are as cooperative as the unidentified customer beside Berry, who is wearing a derby hat in the hardware's doorway. Note the olden kerosene street lamp. (Marleen Hansen Collection.)

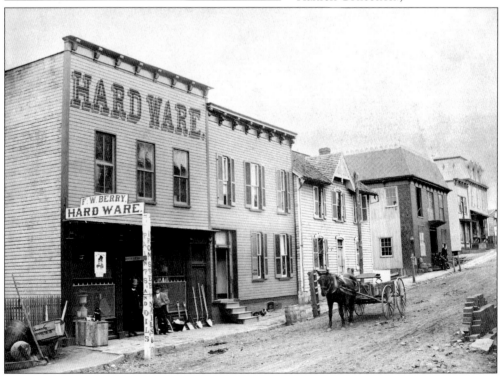

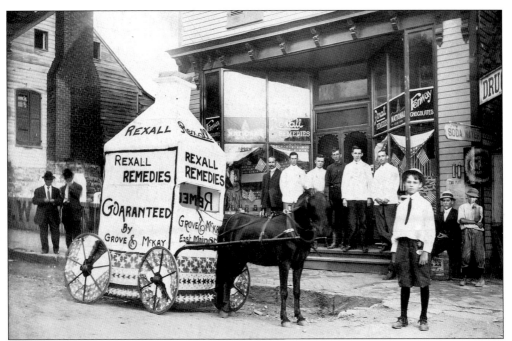

A Grove and McKay buggy was decorated in patriotic style in this scene around 1910. In 1887, Dr. Frank W. Grove purchased this drug store at the corner of Main and Broad Streets in Luray from G.W. Haines, renaming it East End Drug Store. Henry R. McKay, Dr. Grove's first employee, was a partner from 1893 to 1930, when he bought out Dr. Grove's interest and made his son William a partner. William, with the pony, later became the sole proprietor following the death of his father, seen at center in black. (*Page News and Courier* Collection.)

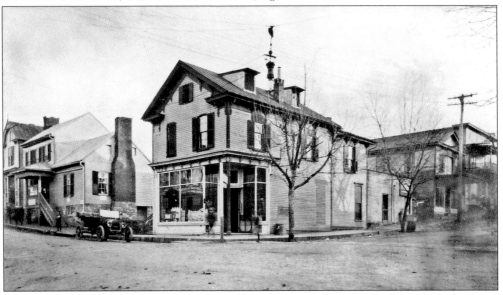

By this time, Grove and McKay had moved their drug store business, and W.G. Fitch's Store opened here. Long overdue electric lights had been installed throughout the town by now, and the people of Luray could not be happier. The *Page News* and *Page Courier*, two local newspapers merging in 1911, would ultimately locate in the building at far right. (Ben Ritter Collection.)

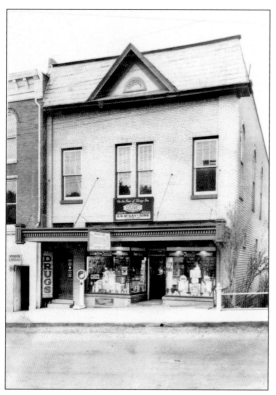

The Luray YMCA originally occupied this building in 1887, and local sculptor Herbert Barbee once had his studio here. Moving his drug store here in 1928 from its origins across East Main, Henry McKay took on his son William as partner, renaming the store McKay and Son. In 1901, a soda fountain installed in the old Grove and McKay Drug Store became a popular attraction, also serving its successor, Butler's Pharmacy. (Nick Smith Collection.)

In 1907, the original Fairview Grocery was pulled several hundred yards eastward to the location seen in this April 1964 photograph. Pictured here, from left to right, are Joe Judd, Martha (Spitler) Flemming (present owner with her husband Dennis), Ruth and Landon Spitler, Charlie Spitler, Dallas Fox (on horse), and an unidentified construction worker. Due to road improvements, a third store, after nearly 100 years of operation, was erected in 1991. (Ruth Spitler Collection.)

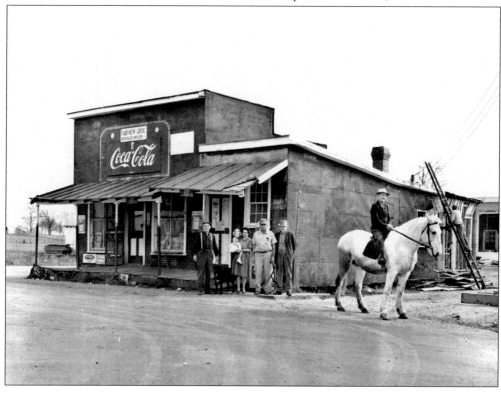

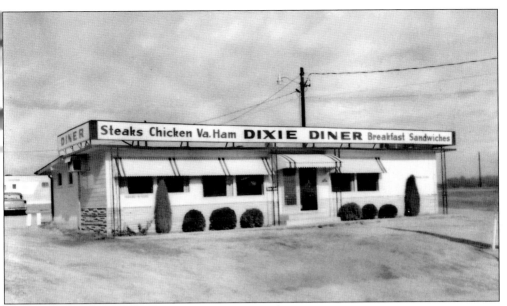

Operated by Jim and Helen Bradford, this was a favorite East Main Street diner for years in Luray. Their main menu was clearly posted to all with breakfast, lunch, and dinner served. (Dan Vaughn Collection.)

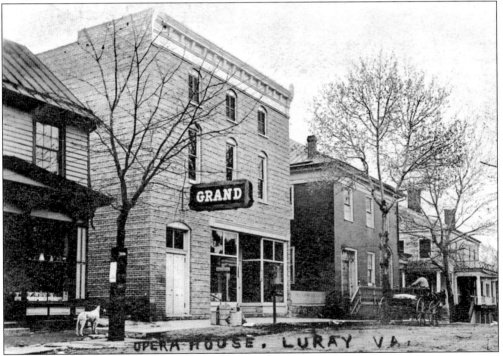

The Grand Opera House on Luray's West Main Street was the scene of local entertainment until the 1930s. Its lighted sign would seem almost surreal at a time when horses, wagons, and dirt streets remained. Opening around 1905, the Grand Opera House was located upstairs in the A.W. McKim Pharmacy, which was established in 1868. The pharmacy, located in the old Virginia Hotel, continues its business until this day. (Dan Vaughn Collection.)

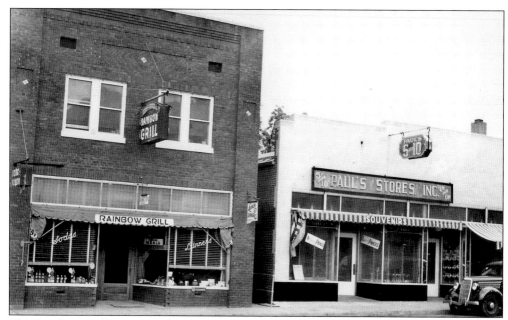

The Rainbow Grill was one of Luray's leading restaurants, while Paul's Stores Five and Dime made for popular variety shopping when both opened in 1937. They were located in what seemed to be an ever-changing site for business on the northeast side of Main Street Bridge. For its second anniversary in 1939, Rainbow Grill owners Mr. and Mrs. C.L. Fake offered souvenirs to women and children, while supposedly the only thing men received was the bill. (Dan Vaughn Collection.)

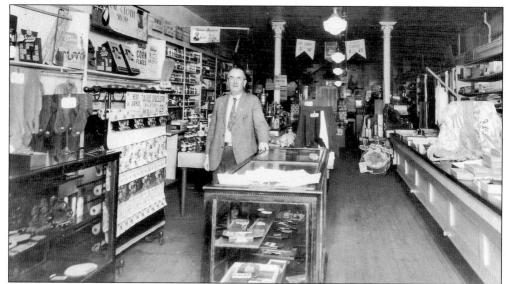

Grove and Bro., initially established in Massanutten near White House Bridge in 1873 by Emanuel Grove and Civil War veterans John W. and Charles H. Grove, moved to Luray in the mid-1880s. John's sons Arthur, one-time Luray postmaster and shown here in the late 1930s, and his brother Harry ran this general merchandise store, the present-day Luray Copy Service. Arthur and Harry's uncle, Dr. Frank W. Grove, partnered Grove and McKay Drug Store. (Ann Vaughn Collection.)

Four

SCHOOL DAYS AND
CHURCH PRAISE

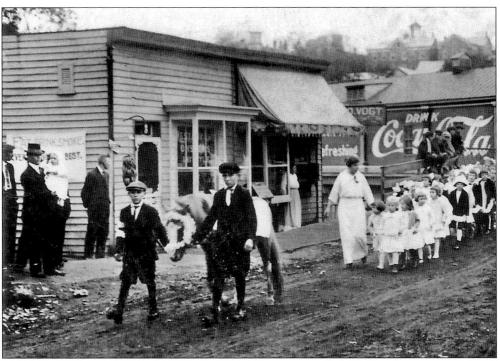

Parades have always been a popular entertaining pastime. Here, children from county schools march east past the photographer in the annual School Days Parade on Main Street in Luray, where a restaurant advertises, "Oysters, Any Style." The number of students in Page was growing, and consolidation would soon take place, bringing to an end the era of the small, one-room schoolhouse. (Peggy Miller Collection.)

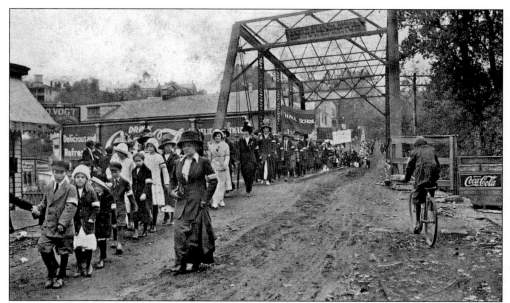

Color-coded armbands helped to identify these formally dressed students from Page County's one-room schoolhouses as they paraded down Main Street Luray. Hall School, seen crossing the iron Warren Truss Hawksbill Creek Bridge, was located in Shenk Hollow, east of Luray. Behind Hall is Valley View, as well as Stony Man School, which actually had a two-room school in its small village. (Alice Moyer Collection.)

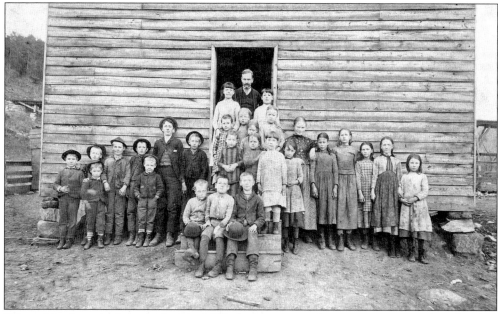

When this photograph was taken in 1889, Ingham was a thriving community, but the slow demise of the Big Gem furnace in Shenandoah would have a devastating effect. Standing in the doorway is John Tampkin, teacher of the one-room schoolhouse, with the Shenandoah Valley Railroad in the background. Operations of the narrow-gauge Ingham Ore Railroad ceased and the rails were removed. The village lost its flagstop and telegraph office, buildings were dismantled, the school closed, and many moved to Shenandoah. (Lucille Painter Collection.)

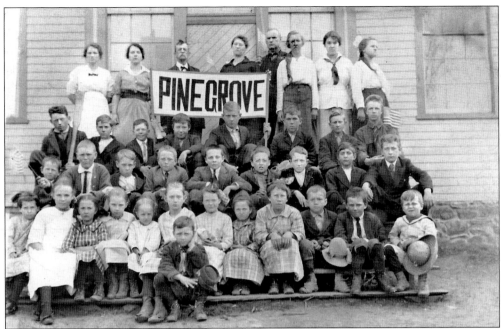

Students of the Pine Grove School in Stanley posed for this photograph in 1916. This was a larger two-room schoolhouse located near St. George's Episcopal Church in Pine Grove Hollow. Martin's Gazetteer of Virginia, in their *Business Directory of Page County*, listed over 70 one- and two-room schoolhouses in this county alone. The early churches usually provided a schoolhouse, and the pastor was frequently the teacher. (Frances Gray Collection.)

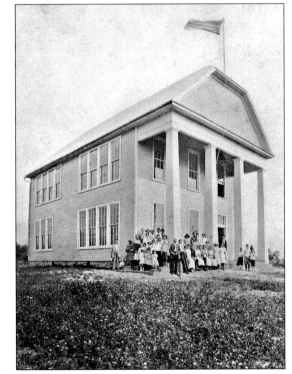

This early view of Rileyville School, taken around 1910 by the Frensley Studio of Luray, shows a rather large four-room schoolhouse that also contained a stage. John Kibler of Springfield was the principal, and school was taught through the ninth grade. When Springfield School was built, the school at Rileyville was discontinued and later torn down. (Anne Stephens Collection.)

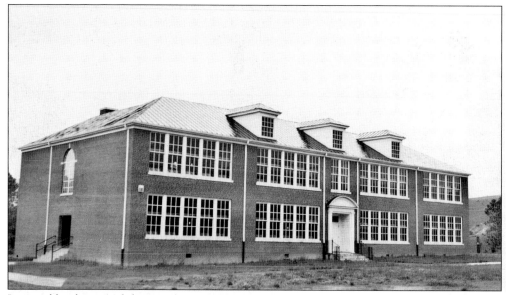

Initiated by the consolidation of many Page County one-room schools, Springfield Elementary was constructed in the late 1930s. Overall, Compton, Rileyville, Vaughn Summit, and Kimball-area students now had a new school, seen here in this 1940 photograph. (Library of Virginia Collection.)

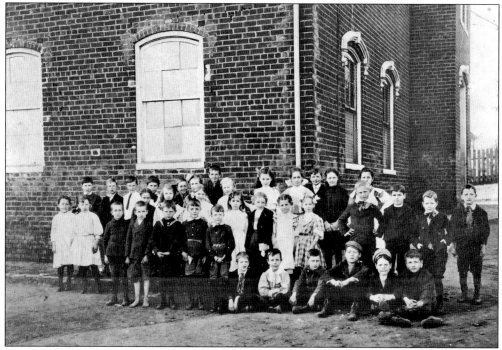

C.L. Proctor was awarded the contract to build a three-story brick building for a graded school. Construction began in May 1881. Originally called Luray Graded School, its first high-school graduation took place in 1903, when Emmett Rankin became its first and only graduate that year. Classes continued here until 1930, when a new school was built. (Phyllis Batman Collection.)

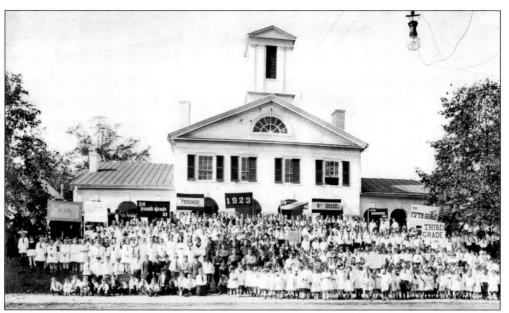

The entire student body of the Luray Graded and High School walked across Court Street for this photograph, taken in front of the Page County Courthouse around 1923. In the center, dressed in black, are the boys' football and girls' basketball teams. From 1903 to 1950, the school had only 11 grade levels. When an additional grade was added, it caused the absence of any graduation ceremonies in 1951. (Dan Vaughn Collection.)

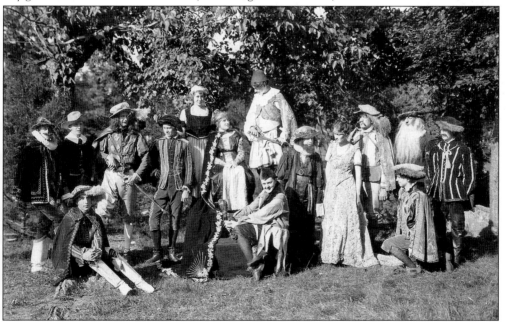

The Luray High School Class of 1918 posed in full costume for a production of Shakespeare's *A Midsummer Night's Dream* in this photograph. Ed Lauck, former editor of the *Page News and Courier*, is among the cast, as well as Mary Grove, seated at center, who played the impish character of Puck, or Robin Goodfellow. Grove would later teach at Luray High School. (*Page News and Courier* Collection.)

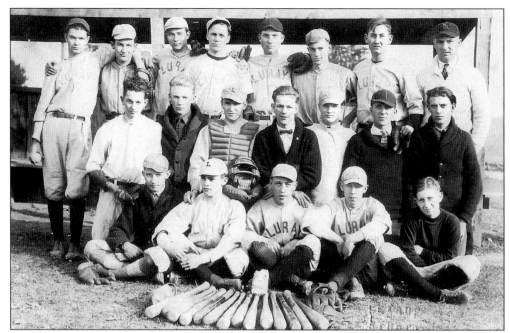

The League Studios of Luray photographed the 1925 Luray Baseball Team. From left to right are (front row) Raymond Shifflet, Carl Kauffman, Osborne Campbell, Albert "Hap" Heiser, and Charles H. Price; (middle row) John Booton, Oscar Brubaker, Randolph Dovel, Rex Knipple, Charles A. Hall, Floyd Kauffman, and Earl Duncan; (back row) Leo Dovel, Earl Kauffman, Abram Brubaker, Blain Burgess, Henry Gander, Dan Yager, Charles Barrett, and coach Leo Strickler. (Becky George Collection.)

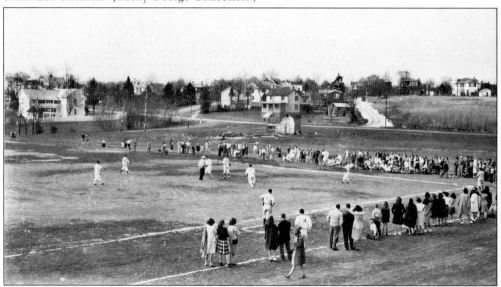

At the time that Luray High School's opening baseball game of 1947 was underway, housing east of Deford Avenue had yet to materialize. Luray Avenue had been laid out as a popular carriage drive when the Luray Inn opened. Running parallel with the first base line, it went past Lee's Lake, built by the railroad in 1890 as an attraction of the inn. Remnants of the lake are still visible on present-day Blue Ridge Avenue. (Lloyd Kibler Collection.)

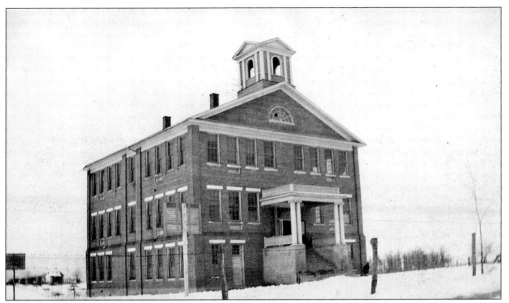

The three-story brick Stanley High School was a commanding structure when it opened on September 20, 1897. A number of leading and enterprising citizens of Stanley had worked to secure a good school for their town. Prof. B.B. White was the principal, aided by a competent corps of assistants. (Dan Vaughn Collection.)

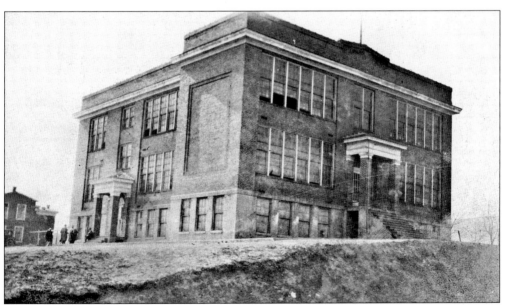

The two-story school, shown at far left, was erected on Third Street in Shenandoah in 1884. When it became inadequate, the cornerstone was laid to the east in 1916 for the new brick 12-room Shenandoah School. The school's first graduating class, in 1918, had six members. In 1928, a twin structure designated as the high school was built. Later, the 1916 portion, shown here, would burn, but it was rebuilt. (Library of Virginia Collection.)

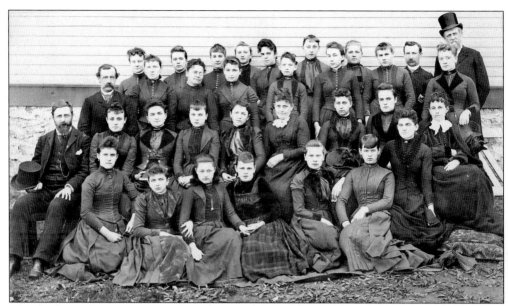

Von Bora College, a finishing school for girls, was named after Martin Luther's wife, Katherine Von Bora. When it opened in 1882 as Girls Home School, classes were first held in Court Street's Luray Graded School. A new college building, financed by B.F. Deford, owner of the Luray Tannery, was completed on Deford Avenue in August 1884. Rev. J.I. Miller, principal, is in the upper right corner in this 1890 photograph. A set of circumstances forced its closure in 1894. (*Page News and Courier* Collection.)

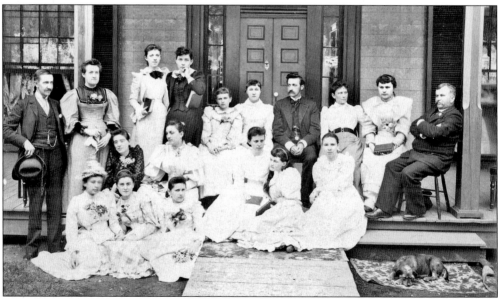

In January 1890, the Legislature of Virginia passed an act "to empower the principal of the Luray Female Institute to grant diplomas." Nearly 50 young ladies attended Prof. M.M. Hargrove's institute that inaugural year, and graduation ceremonies were held June 9 at Luray Baptist Church. Sitting at the head of the South Court Street plank walkway is a graduating class with Professor Hargrove at center and Rev. H.M. Wharton, president, at right. (*Page News and Courier* Collection.)

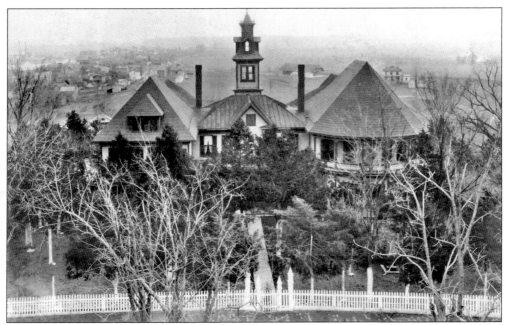

Fog shrouds the town in this 1890s view of Luray College on South Court Street. Known as "Cliff Cottage," it was built by Nicholas Yager for his daughter Mary Overall Yager Jordan. The college, opened on September 18, 1889, would initially operate as the Luray Female Institute. In 1895, Rev. H.M. Wharton purchased the school, and the name changed to accommodate young boys, but with the old name ingrained, this never occurred. (Dan Vaughn Collection.)

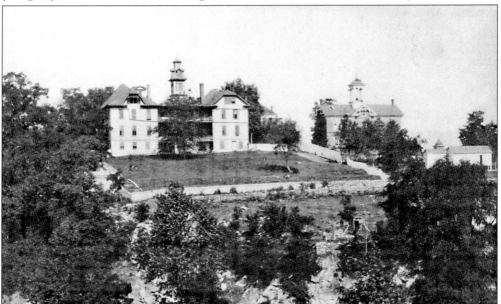

Contractor C.L. Proctor built both Luray College on the left and the adjacent Luray Graded School. In the 1890s, students in advanced grades, referred to as pay pupils, had to purchase their upper-grade privileged education. Public schooling increasingly extended to the high school level, leading to the demise of the private institutes, academies, and colleges that had sprung up in Page County during this era. (June Gochenour Collection.)

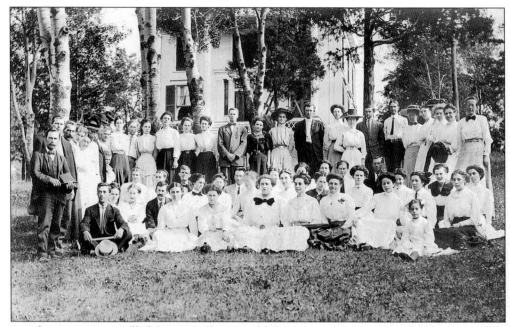

Another institution called Luray College would later open but this time on Aventine Hill, where the Mimslyn Inn is situated. The college only functioned from 1925 to 1927 under Pres. John Booton, seen at right with a black tie. The building was constructed in 1852 by Peter Brock Borst, a Page County commonwealth attorney and state delegate and the first president of the Shenandoah Valley Railroad. His daughter Elizabeth named the home for one of the Seven Hills of Rome. (Dan Vaughn Collection.)

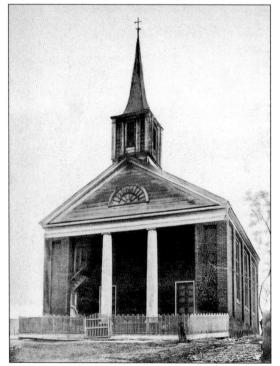

Mt. Carmel Baptist Church, built in 1849, was more commonly known as Broad Street Baptist. Blanche Stover and Herbert Barbee, sculptor of the East End Monument, were married here. In 1881, the trains came and so did the noise. With streets on all sides, caverns hacks and steam whistles, this became rather bothersome during services. The Broad Street Y would remain when the Confederate monument was erected. (Dan Vaughn Collection.)

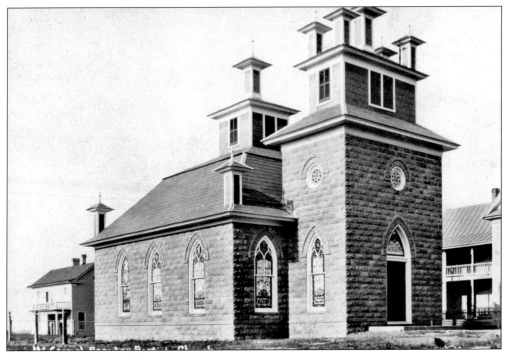

In 1910, Mt. Carmel Regular Baptist Church was built on the corner of Cave Street and Deford Avenue. A 1909 court case settled a split, where, oddly, all members continued to use the same Broad Street building for almost 20 years, alternating Sundays. This was Mt. Carmel's third location since the church was initially established in 1812. The original building was just beyond the southernmost end of South Bank Street. (*Page News and Courier* Collection.)

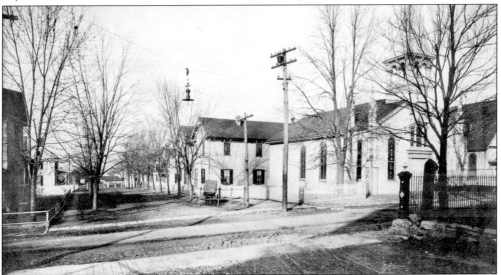

This quaint view of North Deford Avenue in Luray was taken around 1905. Electric lights have finally taken the place of the old kerosene lamps, as well as Stover's acetylene types. Pastor John N. Stirewalt preached the first service here on March 5, 1876, the year of St. Mark's Lutheran Church's organization. Seen directly behind the church is the Von Bora College. (*Page News and Courier* Collection.)

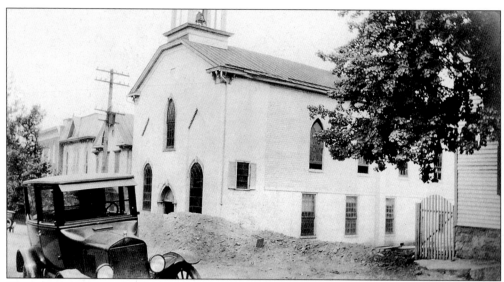

This white, one-story brick church on Luray's Main Street was built in 1844 and organized as the Regular Baptist Church of Christ. Christened the Luray Baptist Church, the name would later change again, to Main Street Baptist. In 1922, an adjacent lot and building were purchased to extend the site for construction of a new house of worship, and that July, the cornerstone was laid for the present church. (Millie Gochenour Collection.)

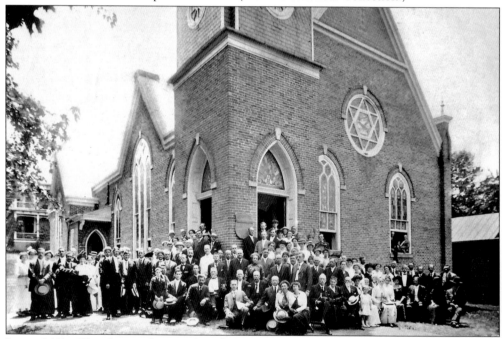

Luray M.E. Church members gathered for this portrait around 1900 in front of the congregation's third church building, located at the corner of Main and Broad Streets. With the first one destroyed in the Civil War and the second torn down, the cornerstone was laid here on August 3, 1899, and dedicated on June 22, 1900. After being virtually destroyed by fire on November 15, 1931, it was rebuilt with native bluestone, reopening on November 13, 1932. (Dan Vaughn Collection.)

Five

WORKING ON
THE RAILROAD

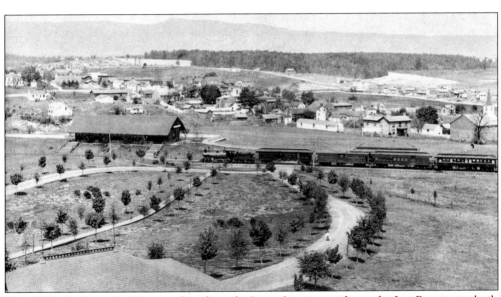

This 1883 photograph of Luray, taken from the Luray Inn tower, shows the Inn Restaurant built by the Shenandoah Valley Railroad just two years earlier. Overflow lunch crowds were served at the home of Mann Spitler, Luray's depot agent, who lived just south of the restaurant. Luray's first and only daily newspaper, the *Luray Times*, was published in its basement. Also seen in this image are the Luray Graded School, at top left; a single-lane bowling alley, right of center; Mt. Carmel Baptist Church at far right; and the original Luray Station, its top protruding from immediately behind the stopped Shenandoah Valley passenger coaches. The restaurant, commonly confused with the 1907 depot, only operated a few years. It was later purchased by the Page Milling Company, moved to the current-day Inn Lawn Park, and finally dismantled in 1946. (Warren and Penny Smith Collection.)

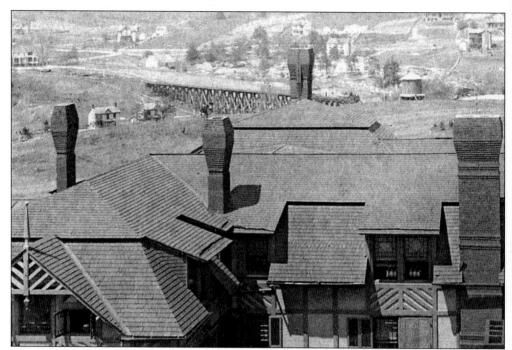

The wooden trestles of the Shenandoah Valley Railroad were in dire need of replacement, especially when the additional trains and heavier engines of the N&W started operating on the line. One of the most disastrous wrecks in the history of the railroad occurred May 31, 1891, at Opossum Hollow Crossing, south of Rileyville. Hawksbill Creek Overpass, seen in background, would not be replaced until November 1900. (Warren and Penny Smith Collection.)

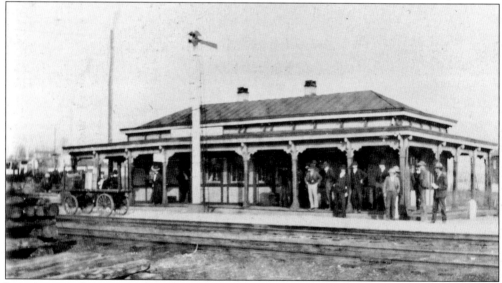

Luray's original passenger depot was completed in the spring of 1881, with Mann Spitler as its first depot agent. With a new walkway and platform constructed in 1897, Luray Station had served the town well when this rare April 1906 photograph was taken. But with the increase of caverns visitors, a larger station would be built shortly thereafter just south of here, where the old Luray Inn Restaurant once stood. (Virginia Historical Society Collection.)

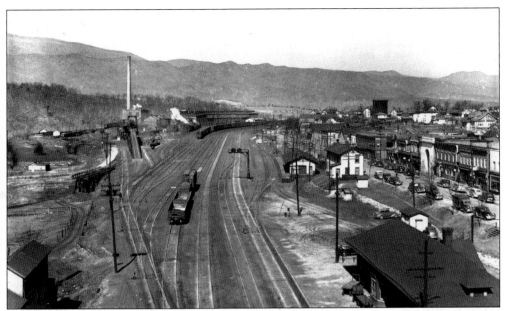

This was Shenandoah. The town revolved around the railroad, and at one time was bigger than Luray. Landowners of Port Republic, Virginia, had rejected a proposal to locate the railroad's divisional headquarters there, and Page County's faltering commitment to issue bonds to the railroad was a deciding factor to build here. And so the Shenandoah Valley Railroad commenced with the construction of Shenandoah Yard. (Virginia Tech Special Collections.)

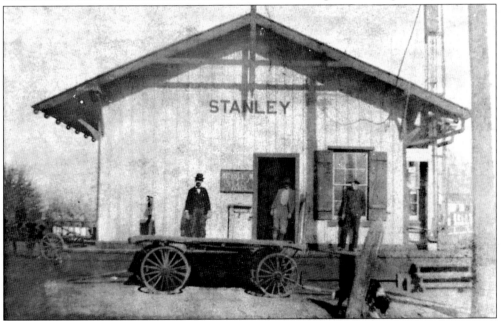

When the railroad was built through Page in 1881, Marksville was a thriving community. With all the railroad could offer, the people gravitated one mile west to this point, and the town of Stanley emerged. In fact, the newly established Marksville Station Post Office was in operation for only one year. One of the railroad company's principal objectives was to develop the mineral resources along the western slopes of the Blue Ridge Mountains. (Pioneer Bank Collection.)

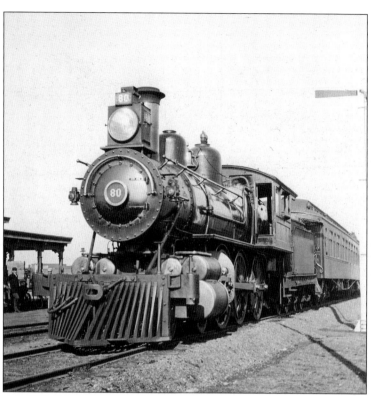

An N&W 2-8-0 steam locomotive makes a stop at Luray Station in this Pancoast glass plate image taken in November 1895. The Liberty Bell, traveling from Philadelphia to the Charleston Exposition, would pass through Luray on January 7, 1902, when the train struck a freight in the night fog stopped to enter a siding. The crew was killed and two baggage cars caught fire, but the bell, undamaged, would continue on by morning. (George Eastman House Collection.)

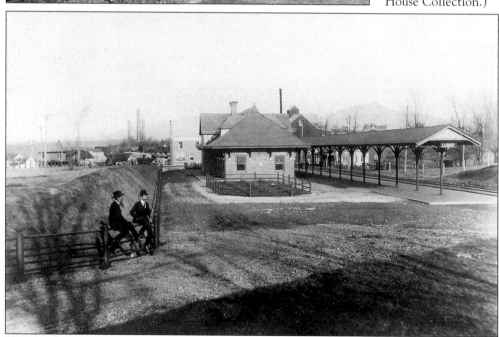

Shortly after the construction of Luray's second station, two unidentified men, waiting for the arrival of an afternoon passenger train, posed in this 1907 photograph. In converting for freight, a south end addition was added around 1940. Seen in the distance are the smokestacks of Deford Tannery, at left, and Page Milling, at center. (*Page News and Courier* Collection.)

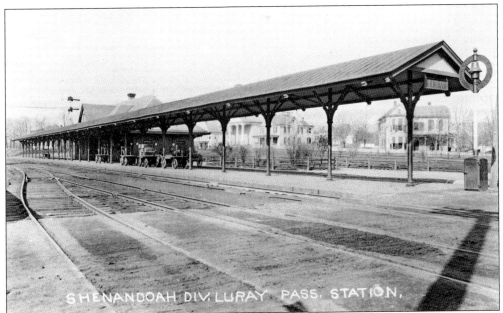

SHENANDOAH DIV. LURAY PASS. STATION.

On March 24, 1881, two railroad construction crews met just north of Deford Tannery, and Mann Almond of Luray drove the final spike to connect the line from Hagerstown to Waynesboro Junction. The first train to make the complete trip south would pass through Luray on April 18. A much-needed canopy served well for the onslaught of passengers, though the north end would be destroyed when a freight car derailed in 1939. (Virginia Tech Special Collections.)

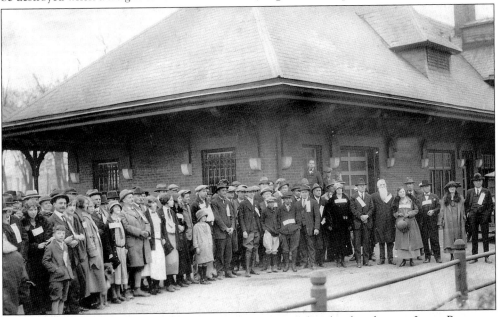

These excursionists posed for the League Studio of Luray shortly after the new Luray Passenger Station opened on February 5, 1907. Designed by N&W chief engineer Charles S. Churchill, it was built to replace the smaller, initial depot, which had become inadequate. Partially burned on June 9, 1908, it would be back in service by the end of September. (*Page News and Courier* Collection.)

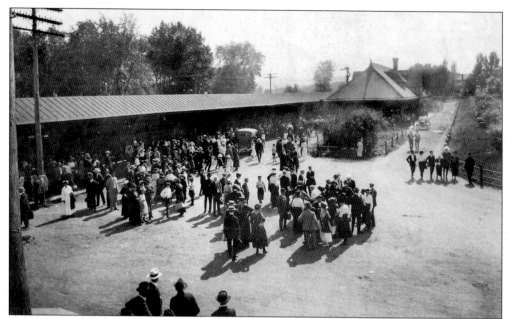

This was a typical afternoon at Luray Station with the large influx of excursionists who came to tour Luray Caverns. On one occasion, 9,000 visitors were conducted through the caverns in a single day. Historian Harry Strickler once said of the caverns, "We know from its wonderful beauty that a Master Architect planned and fashioned its construction, decorated and painted its walls, fluted its columns and carved its friezes, hung its draperies and embellished its ceilings." (*Page News and Courier* Collection.)

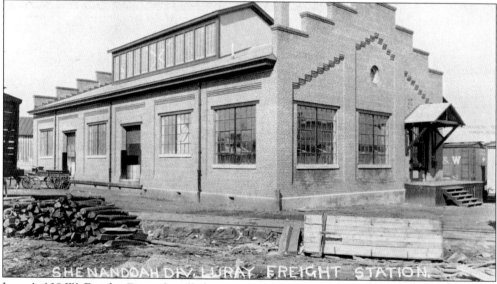

Luray's N&W Freight Depot handled enormous amounts of leather from Deford Tannery during World War I. This photograph dates from April 11, 1917. W.D. Leach, N&W's local freight agent, announced in December 1952 that the station would close, with subsequent freight business consolidated at the recently converted passenger station in Luray. The Southern States Cooperative moved here from their Rosser Drive location in January 1953. (Virginia Tech Special Collections.)

Time Freight 96, entering from the south, crosses the plate girder over U.S. Route 340 in Luray. The N&W Railroad was the last commercially operated steam railroad in America. Famed photographer O. Winston Link captured this image, one of his most famous, of children playing in Luray's Hawksbill Creek. The children, from left to right, are Jerry Judd, his sister Marjorie, Reggie and Ginger Judd, Barry Good, and Tommy Judd. Link gave each a silver dollar for posing. (O. Winston Link Museum Collection, Roanoke, Virginia.)

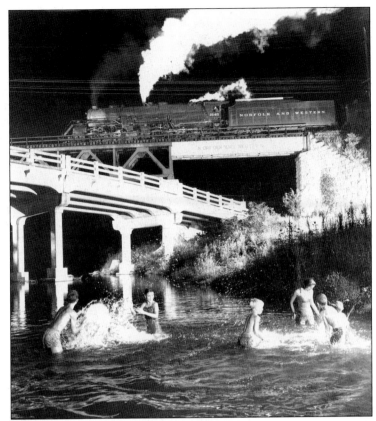

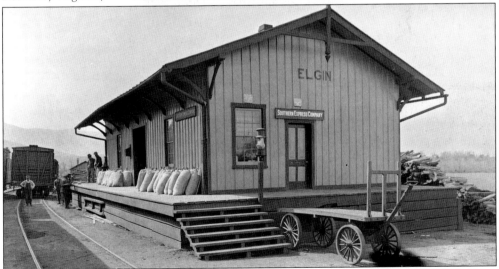

Page County's first depot north of Luray, Kimball, seen here in 1917, was originally named after Frederick J. Kimball, Shenandoah Valley Railroad's president. The N&W would acquire this line in 1890, and with a Kimball already in existence on their Ohio extension, Kimball Depot was renamed Elgin. Freight traffic had increased five-fold by this time. The post office would retain the Kimball name, but sadly, the depot and post office closed in 1952 and 1954 respectively. (Virginia Tech Special Collections.)

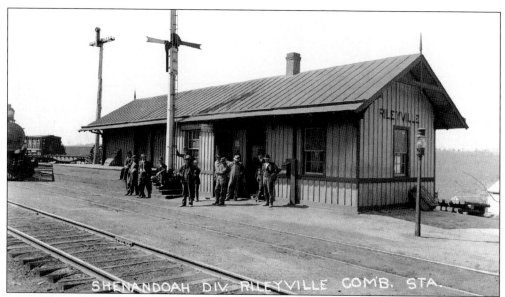

Originally built in 1890, this was Rileyville's third station, the first two burning in 1893 and 1909. When local N&W agent R.L. Rodgers operated the depot, the 50,000-gallon water tank south of town was filled by a pump-house at Jeremiah's Run. With the railroad presenting a loss, their request for closure was granted. And so, on June 1, 1952, against the favor of the citizens, Rileyville Depot closed and was dismantled. (Norfolk and Western Historical Society Collection.)

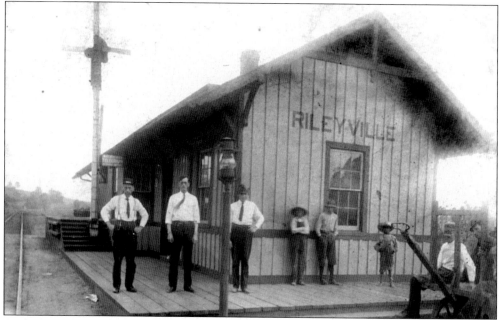

A plank decking had been added at Rileyville when R.L. Rodgers, at center, was photographed with two unidentified employees of the station. A rail steam shovel, doing work at Vaughn's Summit, passed unmanned by the depot after its brakes gave way. It came to a stop on the upgrade opposite Maddox's Store in Compton. In its wild run of five miles, no opposition was encountered and no damage resulted. (Phil and Kay Mims Collection.)

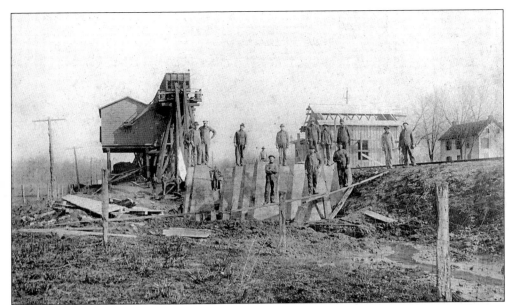

These workers posed for this early 1900s photograph of the construction of a railroad water tank in Shenandoah. N&W's larger articulated Mallets could hold as much as 30,000 gallons of water in their tenders, so tanks needed to be in close proximity to one another. (Karen Miller Collection.)

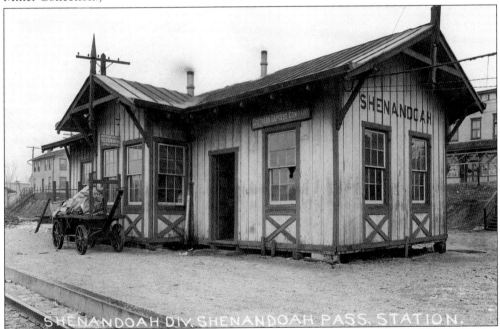

Shenandoah's original passenger station was still in operation when this photograph was taken in 1917. Built in 1880 by the Shenandoah Valley Railroad, it had seen better days. An elaborate depot was proposed, but with SVRR's foreclosure and the 1890s depression, it never materialized. Shenandoah Valley's pre-operations president, William Milnes Jr. (Milnes, Virginia), the 1881 president, Frederick J. Kimball (Kimball, Virginia), and Joseph Sands (Sands, Virginia) would all pass here. (Virginia Tech Special Collections.)

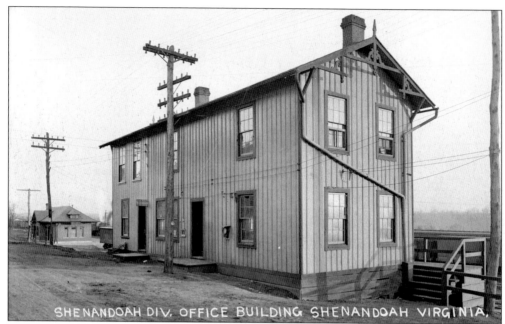

SHENANDOAH DIV. OFFICE BUILDING SHENANDOAH VIRGINIA,

This image embodies a different railroad than we know today. The N&W's Shenandoah Division operations were directed from here. The building housed the telegraph and freight offices, with railroad passes issued upstairs. By now the N&W brick passenger station, long overdue, had been built and would later be converted to the freight office. (Norfolk and Western Historical Society Collection.)

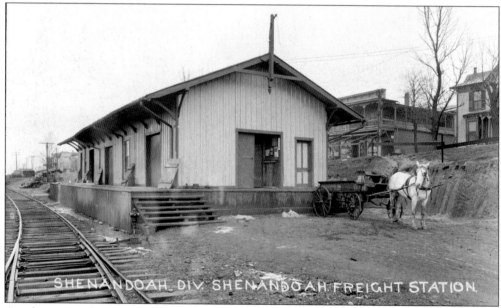

SHENANDOAH DIV. SHENANDOAH FREIGHT STATION.

Another original 1880 Shenandoah Valley structure was the divisional freight station at Shenandoah. The station was relatively moderate in size, considering the railroad town that Shenandoah was, but most of the freight moved by rail here was bulk material loaded on spurs and shipped directly, bypassing this building. The transportation of the day in this 1917 photograph was still horse with buckboard wagon. (Norfolk and Western Historical Society Collection.)

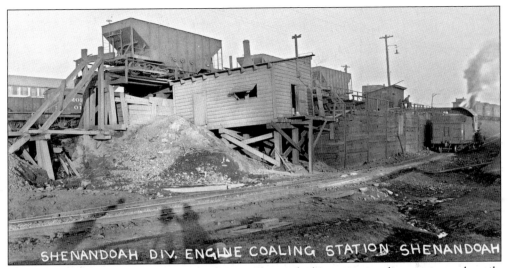

SHENANDOAH DIV. ENGINE COALING STATION SHENANDOAH

A line of N&W coal cars awaits unloading at Shenandoah's engine coaling station, a heavily used facility in Shenandoah Yard. Enormous amounts of water and coal were needed to power the large Mallets that the N&W was now operating. This southbound locomotive, just fully loaded, is returning to the switchyard in this 1917 view. N&W's Shenandoah YMCA can be seen at upper left. (Virginia Tech Special Collections.)

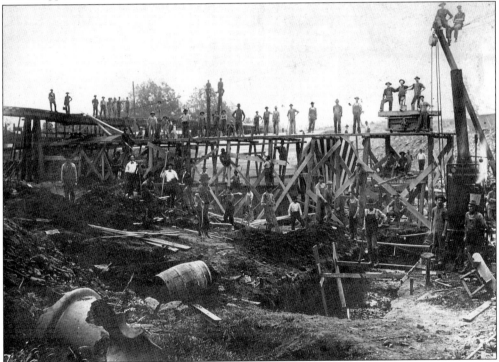

With N&W's heavier train traffic and the need for a second rail, construction commenced on this arched Maryland Avenue tunnel in Shenandoah. Smoke puffs from a steam hoist that lifts concrete to a waiting rail cart. Replacing an earlier wooden structure, it too would later be "flat-topped" and shored up in 1918. The railroad, with surveyors on site, seemed to spare no worker on this necessary project as recorded in this posed scene around 1900. (Allan Rinaca Collection.)

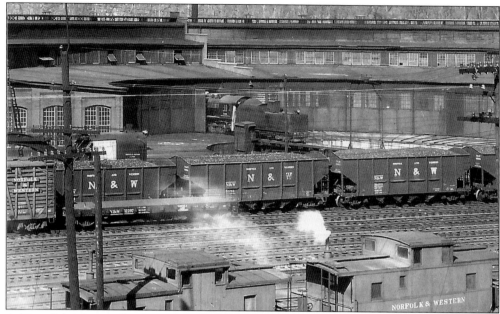

A 21-stall brick roundhouse with a 60-foot turntable constructed in 1892 would prove to be inadequate when the N&W introduced their articulated Mallet locomotives. In 1919, a new roundhouse was constructed, again with 21 stalls, but this time with a 115-foot turntable accommodating N&W's entire stock, as seen in this March 1941 photograph. (*Page News and Courier* Collection.)

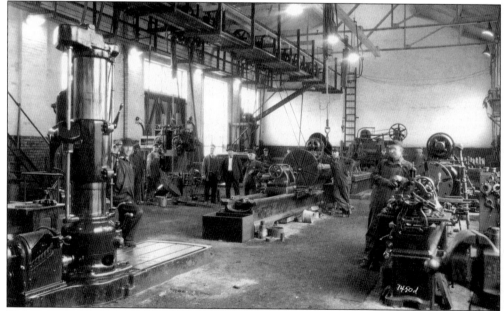

Knowing it was not possible to run a railroad without extensive repair facilities, Milnes's rejection at Port Republic finalized his decision to build the railroad shops at Shenandoah. During peak employment in the "Tremendous Twenties," this Shenandoah industry gave work to over 500 in the vicinity. With the steam era concluding by 1958, all but minimum operations had ended. (Virginia Tech Special Collections.)

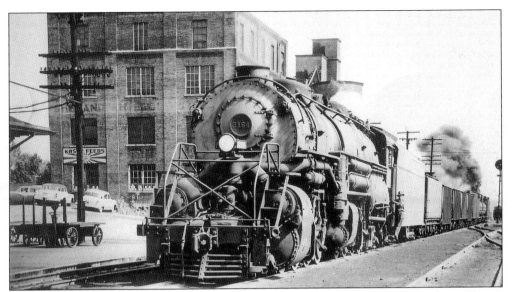

Slowly moving north in Shenandoah Yard, a class Y6a R/N 2164, a 2-8-8-2 Mallet, is overpowered for the short freight it is pulling as it passes by Shenandoah Milling Company in 1956. Steam power had come to an end when the N&W would officially dieselize on February 21, 1957. By now the work in the shops here had been transferred to Roanoke. (Larry Baugher Collection.)

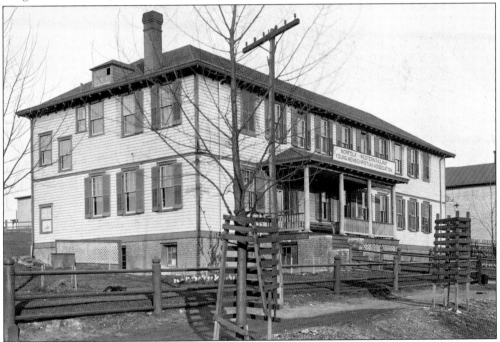

The Shenandoah YMCA, first organized in 1893, rented quarters for 14 years before this 1907 building was constructed. Gospel meetings and Bible classes were held here, as well as meals, rooms, and showers for the members. The building was always open, and over the next 20 years, over 100,000 would pass through its doors. Although no longer a YMCA, the building is still standing. (Virginia Tech Special Collections.)

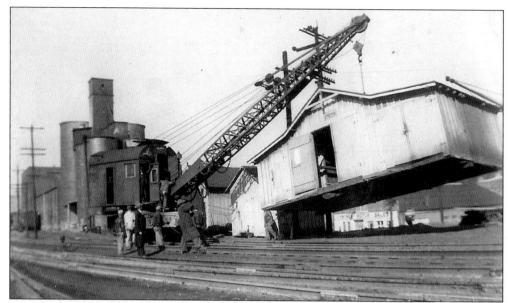

The railroad, from its beginnings, had continually made adaptations to meet the changing needs of the day. Here a rail crane is used in Shenandoah Yard to literally relocate this storage building. (Becky George Collection.)

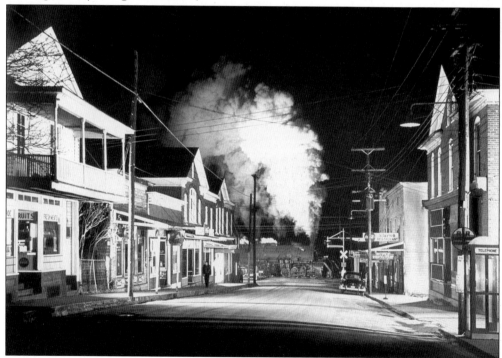

O. Winston Link would continue documenting the steam railroad era in print with this Main Street scene in Stanley. The N&W was very gracious and greatly cooperated to accommodate Link in his work of the mid- to late 1950s. Timing was critical with his nighttime photos. Taken with carefully positioned lighting, the detail was intensified, especially the steam. (O. Winston Link Museum Collection, Roanoke, Virginia.)

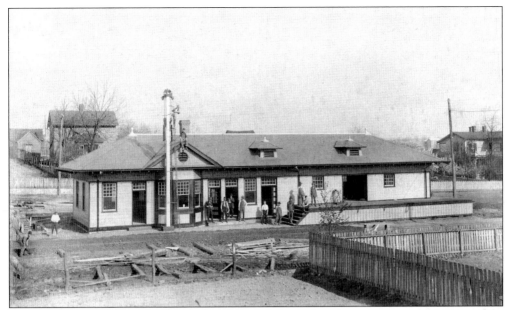

The Stanley Depot was spared from the May 1909 fire only to burn just six months later. This railroad construction crew poses with the new depot that was completed by early spring 1910. N&W regularly anticipated the burning of their depots. In a time when wood heat and ejecting embers from steam locomotives was the mainstay, most Page County depots and siding stations burned at least once. (John Belton Collection.)

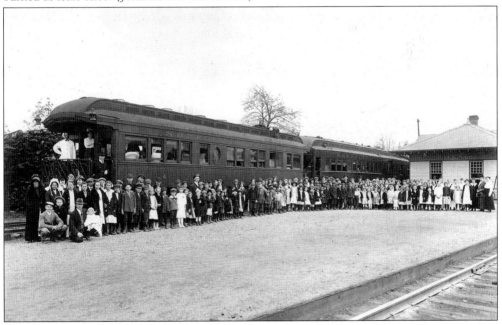

This unidentified group of mostly school-aged children going on an excursion posed at N&W's Stanley Station to have their picture taken in 1917. The railroad porter waits patiently on the southbound passenger. By now the train had become an integral part of the community, and almost everyone had an association with it in some manner. (Virginia Tech Special Collections.)

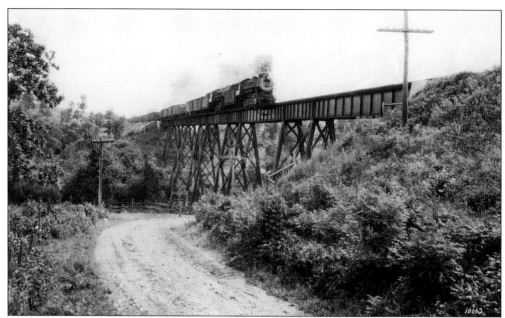

Double-headed 4-8-0's are southbound crossing the pass at Overall, Virginia, in this early 1920s photo. The N&W built this bridge in 1918 as a replacement needed to run the heavier Mallet locomotives they were now routinely using. In 1941, Norfolk and Western took the same precautions as in World War I when they sent troops to guard this, and other, trestles throughout Page County. (Virginia Tech Special Collections.)

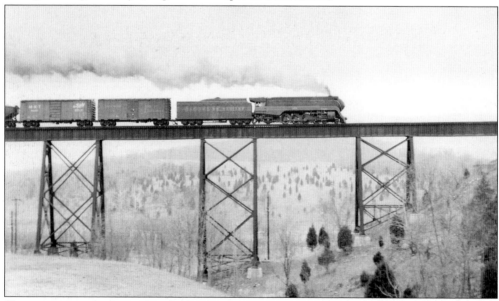

Shown crossing the 1,141-foot bridge at Compton, Virginia, on February 19, 1957, is the last regularly scheduled steam locomotive to pass over the N&W line in Page County. Through a technicality, the northbound streamlined class K2a R/N 129, a 4-8-2, would actually be pulled deadhead back to Roanoke, seeing the steam here for the last time. Compton housed Shenandoah Divisional Headquarters in August 1893, when Superintendent Cook and other railroad officials visited Keyser's Grove. (*Page News and Courier* Collection.)

Six

AT YOUR SERVICE

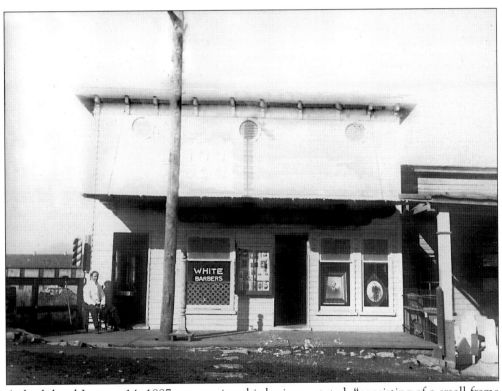

A deed dated January 14, 1887, concerning this business, stated, "consisting of a small frame house now rented as a barber shop . . . east of the bridge on the north side of Main Street. . . ." Housed in this small 1880s structure were White Barbers, Mr. J.H. Bushong's Photographic Gallery, and Bradley Marble and Granite Works. Note the speed bumps here, scrap marble from Bradley Bros. (*Page News and Courier* Collection.)

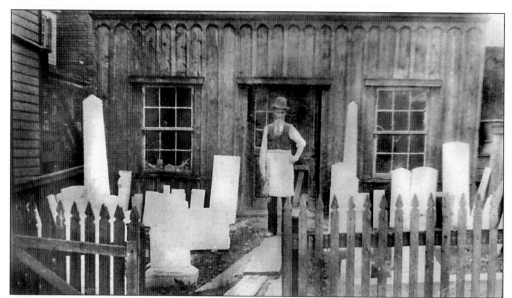

Page County Marble Works proprietor Daniel Fagan, seen here in the early 1880s, was advertised in the *Page Courier* as "The Old Reliable." In 1877, he laid out Green Hill Cemetery in East Luray. The craftsmanship he learned from his father, before moving from Winchester to Luray, is evident there. When Fagan died, his successor, George W. Haines, continued the profession of marble cutting on East Main Street. (Ben Ritter Collection.)

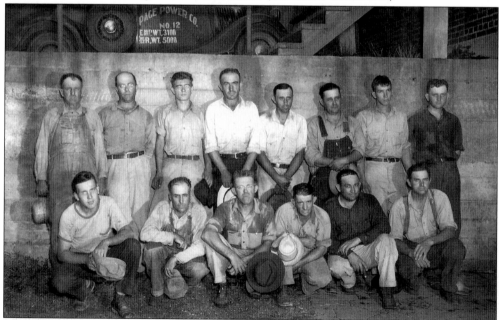

Employees of the Page Power Company posed in the early 1940s after a hard day's work. Pictured from left to right are (front row) Dick Freeland, Bill Rowe, Bob Shenk, Everett Emerson, Drexel Ponn, and Raymond Painter; (back row) Mike Rickard, Bernard Shenk, "Teeny" Donovan, Haywood Nichols, Elmer Hinton, Horace Estep, Billy Miller, and Carson Aleshire. Page Power was incorporated into Potomac Power and Electric in August 1945. (Teeny Donovan Collection.)

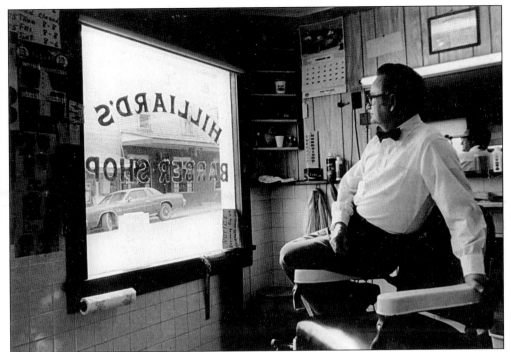

Hilliard's Barber Shop, operated by Emmit Carlton "Buddy" Hilliard, was a Main Street regular for decades in Stanley. Hilliard's father encouraged him as a child to enter the barbering trade after learning to cut hair in the U.S. Army. He later taught four of his brothers this profession, and they ultimately came to help him, beginning in the late 1940s. A notice in the window read, "Beginning August 4th, Haircuts, Flattops, $2.50." (Myrtle Hilliard Collection.)

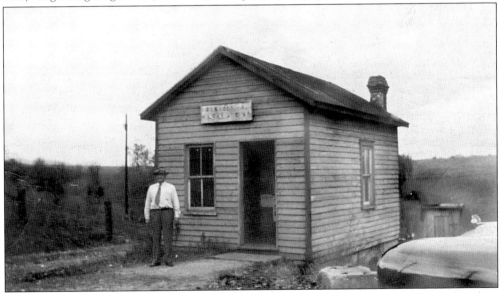

Vernon Good, postmaster at the Rileyville Post Office for over 45 years, poses outside his place of employment. He would use five horses and nine automobiles in the 400,000 miles traveled during his tenure, which began in 1906. Post offices commonly had one name and their community another, as in Cedar Point Post Office in Rileyville. (Karen Cooper Collection.)

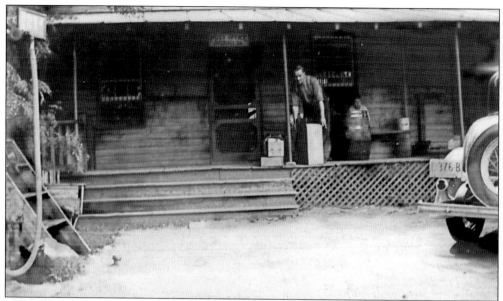

A.L. Rinker, postmaster of the Overall Post Office, is seen here around 1920. Initially operating as Overall from 1881 to 1892, the post office discontinued in 1972. Page County ultimately had 46 different named post offices, many just name changes (though 27 operated simultaneously by 1902) before the Rural Free Delivery system went into effect. The Dashaway Post Office, in the Kimball area, operated for only 12 days. (Jimmy Rinker Collection.)

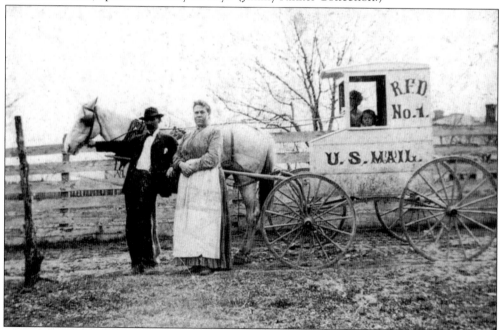

When Daniel F. Holmes, seen here with his family, was awarded the contract as mail carrier on rural delivery route (RFD) No. 1 between Luray and Oak Hill south of Rileyville, he made his first trip on August 1, 1902. A "free delivery" wagon had already arrived, and Holmes informed patrons on the route that they could put up temporary boxes until the iron boxes arrived. (*Page News and Courier* Collection.)

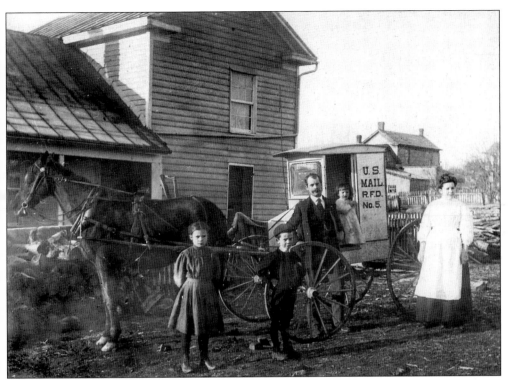

When Rural Free Delivery was initiated in Page County in 1902, it prompted the appointment of local postal carriers. David B. Broyles is seen here around 1907 with his family and the horse-drawn mail wagon he used as a carrier on RFD No. 5. His son Paul B., at center, later became a postal clerk. They are in front of the Broyles home on Mechanic Street. (William and Frances Menefee Collection.)

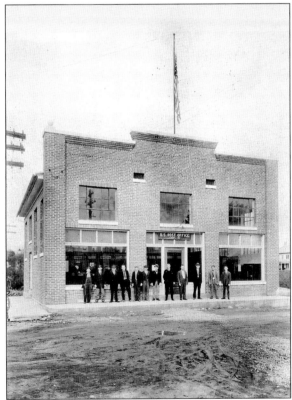

The Luray Post Office, leaving the First National Bank Building in 1926, would move across North Broad Street into this spacious building, their fifth location. Posing in front of the new post office are, from left to right, Hughes Campbell, George Brown, Tom J. Bailey, George Burrill, Ralph Rothgeb, D.B. Broyles, Hallar Beach, Everette Berrey, Jack Beach, Lee Berry, Lloyd Foltz, and Paul B. Broyles. (Dorothy Rothgeb Collection.)

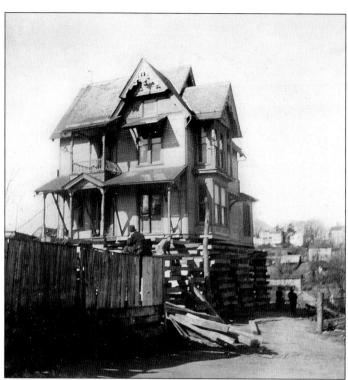

Dr. H.L. Rankin completed this South Broad Street residence in December 1891, and it stood undisturbed for almost 50 years. In 1938, the federal government purchased the land and paid to relocate the house so a new Luray Post Office could be constructed on the site. Miss Willie Reed, resident at the time, had the house moved west near the old Stover gas plant. (Ann Vaughn Collection.)

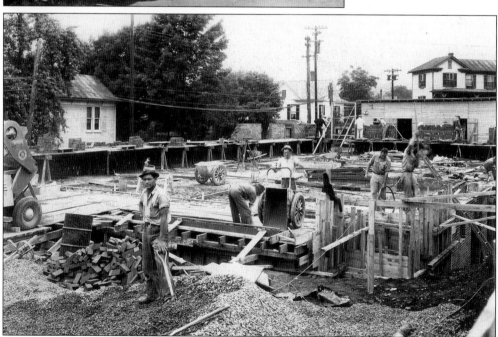

Photographed by contractor Algernon Blair of Montgomery, Alabama, construction was progressing on the new South Broad Street Luray Post Office. Workers had begun pouring concrete by May 27, 1938, when this photograph was taken. Luray's old Commercial Hotel, at upper right, burned in November 2002. To alleviate confusion, Luray initiated the numbering of its houses and businesses in 1896. (Luray Post Office Collection.)

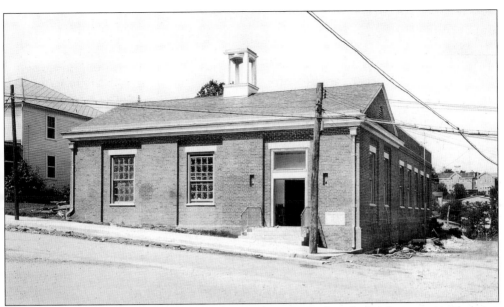

When postal cards originated in 1873, H.C. Fravel purchased the first one sold, being postmarked on May 21 at Luray Post Office on West Main Street. An interior mural painted by Sheffield Kagey of Washington, D.C., was a 1939 Works Progress Administration (WPA) project. Seen at right is the former Luray Graded and High School. This sixth and current location was dedicated on October 10, 1938. (Luray Post Office Collection.)

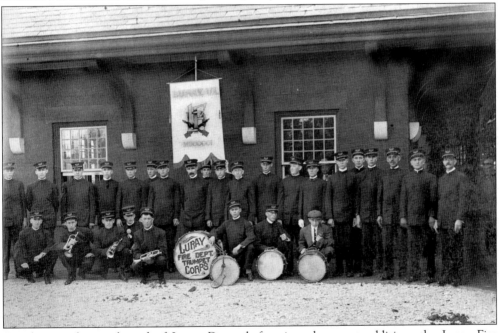

Standing at the south end of Luray Depot before its subsequent addition, the Luray Fire Department Trumpet Corps sports a banner that posts an erroneous Roman numeral date of 1901, the year of their organization. Luray now had a fire department and was proud of it, for fire had destroyed a multitude of business structures and dwellings by the time this photo was taken around 1910. (Mrs. H.T.N. Graves Collection.)

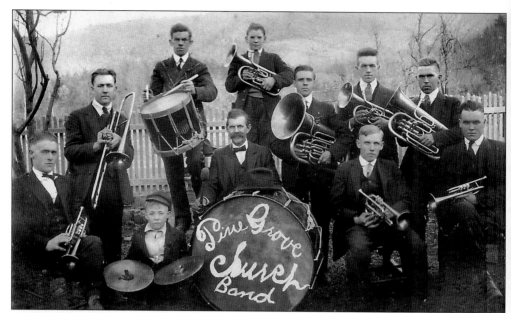

The Pine Grove Church Band posed here in the 1920s. Members included, from left to right, Lloyd Gray, Vernon Jenkins, Carl Pettit, Ivan Pettit, Charles Pettit, Earnest Weakley, Leonard Gray, Everette Weakley, and Lake Southard. The lad in front is Oscar Pettit, and in the center is drummer Herbert Gray. The band once climbed Tanner's Ridge with instruments in hand to perform a Christmas service at the schoolhouse. Many gifts were handed out. (St. George's Episcopal Church Collection.)

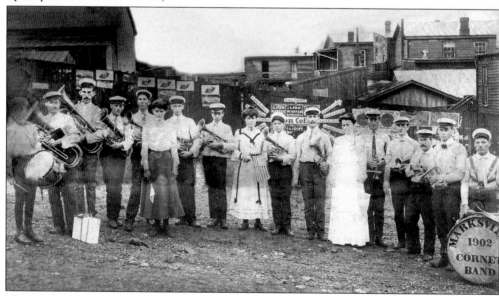

The Marksville Cornet Band, seen here in Shenandoah shortly after they organized in 1902, commonly traveled throughout the county and entertained at social events. Posing with their instruments, from left to right, are Amos Koontz, Hubert Koontz, Seldon Biedler, three unidentified, Jacob Offenbacker, Rufus Kibler, unidentified, Frank Cave, Dock Weakley, unidentified, Harry Hutchinson, Edward Judy, John Graves, Dan Biedler, and Al Hutchinson with the band's bass drum. (Town of Stanley Collection.)

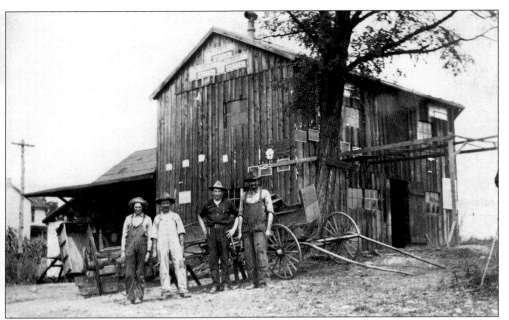

Posed in front of the Ed Cullers Blacksmith Shop in Rileyville are, from left to right, Joe Menefee, James Seekford, unidentified, and Edward C. Cullers. Anything from wagon-wheel bands to barn-door strap hinges was made here, at the northwest corner of the intersection of Rileyville's Main Street and the N&W Railroad. The shop has since been torn down. (Karen Cooper Collection.)

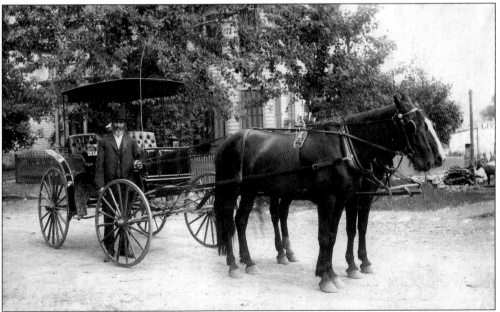

This unidentified hack posed at the turn of the last century, at the intersection of Broad and Main Streets in Luray. The H.R. McKay house, built in 1880, is seen in the background obscured by trees. The H.O. Brubaker Livery Stable, at far right, was newly built in May 1901 and was located on North Broad Street in the rear of the McKay lot. It had previously operated behind Page Valley Bank when on Bank Street. (Richard and Olena Sours Collection.)

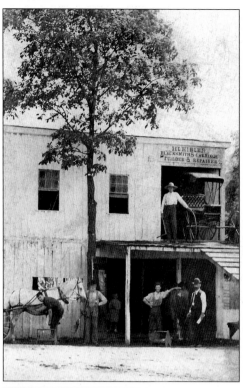

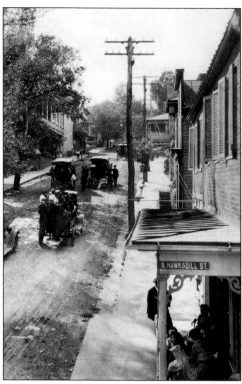

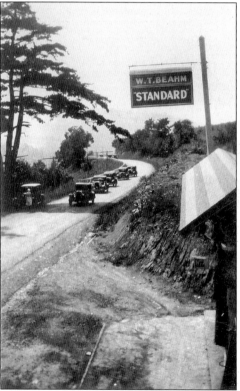

(*Above, left*) This view of the H.L. Kibler Blacksmith Shop clearly shows the work that was performed. The blacksmith work was done below, while carriage repair and repainting were done above. A message to John M. Shaffer of Luray read, "You can get your runabout the last of the week. . . . it is all done now, but not dry yet." (Dan Vaughn Collection.)

(*Above, right*) J.P. Grove and Sons offered buggies at their Zirkle Street establishment, but the new-fangled motorized hacks were much to the advantage of the tourists. From the depot past Broad Street Baptist to Main Street, the road condition was so bad that it became a free advertisement for hacks. (*Page News and Courier* Collection.)

(*Left*) In 1928, Beahm's Standard Oil was located on Lee Highway. William T. Beahm was postmaster of the Beahm Post Office, and he ran his store there until the mid-1930s. When the Shenandoah National Park was established, he moved to Marksville and continued the business his son would operate into the 1960s. (Diana Smith Collection.)

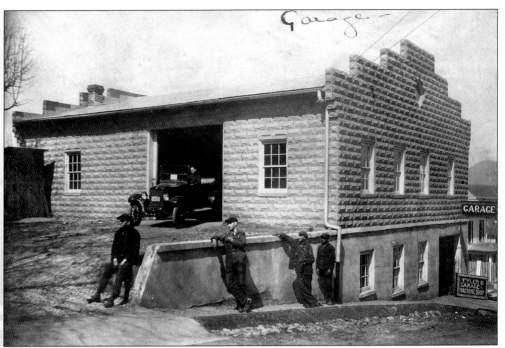

This view taken from North Court Street looking northwest shows Joseph T. Campbell in one of his dealership cars with his employees on their lunch break. Automobiles had become a popular source of transportation, and that necessitated shops such as this. At right are Tyler's Garage and Machine Shop and Massanutten Mountain's Kennedy Peak. (Becky George Collection.)

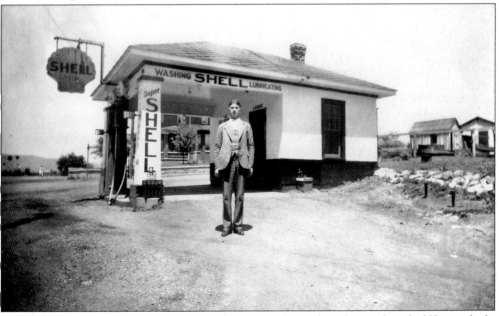

In the 1930 *Bradstreet's Business Directory*, this station, located on the north end of Shenandoah, was listed as "G.A. Stepp, Gasoline &cetera." Pictured here is Claude Stepp, owner Gilbert A. Stepp's brother, at the Stepp Shell Station. Located on the corner of Fourth Street and Denver Avenue, the building was torn down in the 1980s. (*Page News and Courier* Collection.)

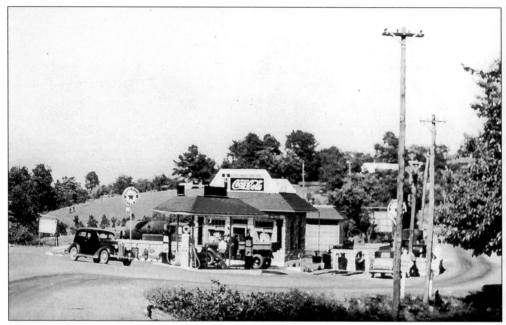

The popular Cave Brothers Service Station in Stanley began operations in 1935, with owners Cletus and Joe Cave Sr. A variety of products were sold, including groceries, Texaco gasoline, Philco radios, Fridgedair appliances, Firestone tires, Case farm tractors, and even Chrysler automobiles. It even became an entryway for visitors to the newly formed Shenandoah National Park. (J.D. Cave Collection.)

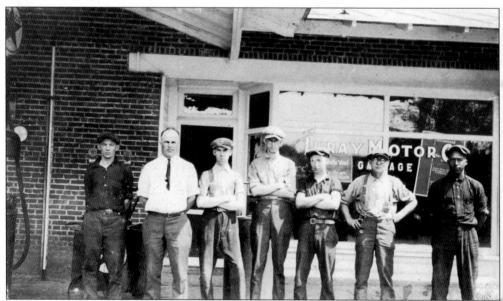

The first automobiles for sale in Page County arrived just before the onset of World War I. E.N. Hershberger established Luray Motor Company, a Ford franchise dealership, in 1914. This 1927 photograph of the employees includes, from left to right, Bill Judd, Maurice Waters, Claude Judd, Harry Cloud, Tony Short, Harper Strickler, and Ike Taylor. (*Page News and Courier* Collection.)

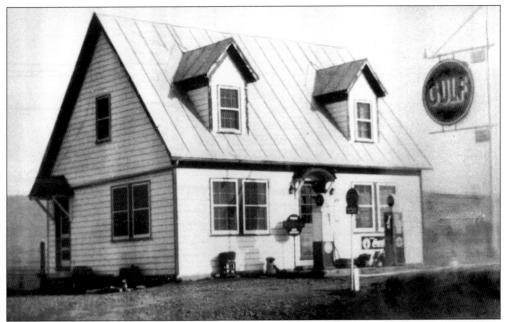

With automobiles came gasoline stations, and Montgomery's Store became a popular stopping point north of Luray. Built in 1939, the building was enlarged or renovated a number of times over the years. The business became the present-day Hope Mills Country Store. (Bill Hope Collection.)

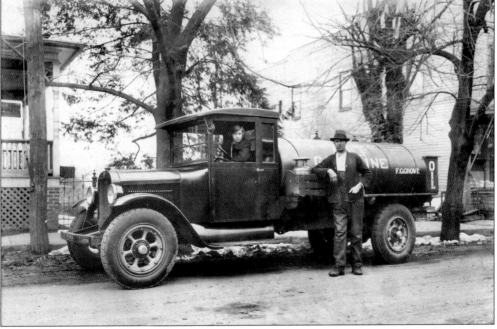

The F.G. Grove Co., established in 1891 to provide kerosene, soon expanded to offer gasoline, coal, oil, cement, and even wagons. In 1911, gasoline sales surpassed kerosene and became Frank Grove's biggest seller. A local inventor, he designed a patented folding umbrella and a bicycle chain brake, both sold in Luray. (Dan Vaughn Collection.)

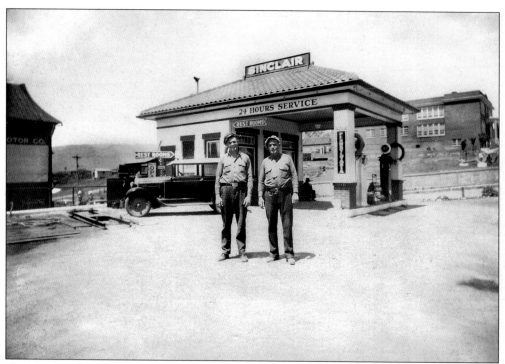

This Sinclair Service Station was located at the corner of Fourth Street and Maryland Avenue in Shenandoah. Jim Orye, seen here on the right with his son Floyd Bernard "Stiff" Orye, purchased the station from W.E. and Clyde Hisey of Hisey Bros. Pharmacy. The Sinclair Oil Corp. had been formed in 1916. The Oryes posed for this photograph in the spring of 1936. (Karen Miller Collection.)

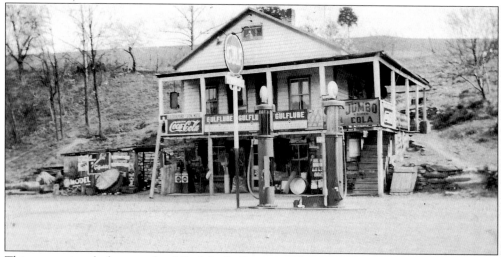

This promotional photograph of Seekford's Store in Alma, Virginia, was taken on April 5, 1938, by Gulf Oil products distributor C.J. Hensley of McGaheysville. Callie David "C.D." Seekford built the store in 1931, and it remained in business until 1991. The porches have been removed and the old hand-crank pumps are gone, but the original store still stands today with additions on each side. (Kristi Painter Hilliard Collection.)

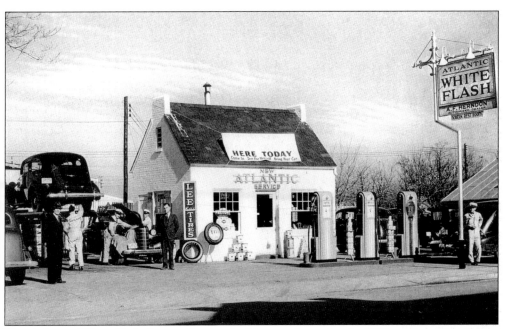

The Atlantic White Flash Service Station had its grand opening in 1938 on East Main Street in Luray. From left to right are distributor C.N. Shannon from Mount Jackson, three unidentified employees, owner Ashby Herndon Sr., and operator Hugh Jenkins. Known as Atlantic Stations east of the Mississippi and Richfield in the west, the company would later nationalize under the name Arco. (Mrs. Robert L. Herndon Collection.)

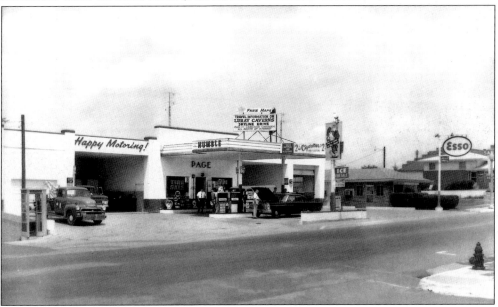

In 1965, this Page Esso Station in Luray was considered the most modern auto service in the county. The parent company, originating as Standard Oil (S.O.), soon realized this could be displayed as Esso. When it was discovered in 1972 that "Esso" meant "stalled car" in Japanese, the company spent $2 million to change its name in the United States to Exxon. (Dan Vaughn Collection.)

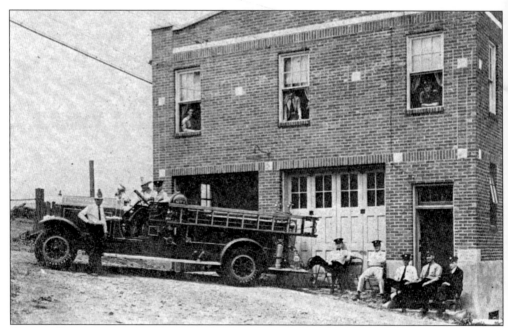

On October 1, 1929, a committee was appointed to confer with the Luray Town Council for the purpose of building a firehouse and buying a fire truck. The firemen, through an immense amount of sacrificial work, raised the total cost. Proper steps were also taken to have the Luray Volunteer Fire Department incorporated. The Vogt Place structure was home for over 60 years. (Cora Frymyer Collection.)

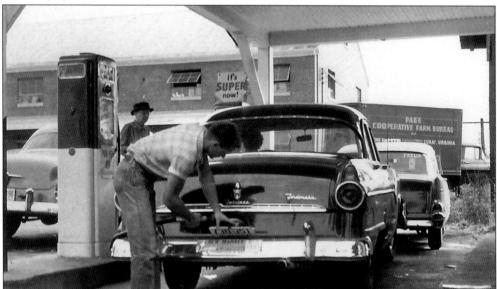

In the late 1950s, the original Page Cooperative Farm Bureau gas station was a small structure with an open oil-changing pit. Here, Glendon Vaughn of Luray fills up a 1955 Ford Fairlane Fordomatic with Pure gasoline as another regular customer watches on. Page Cooperative eventually operated the larger station across Virginia Avenue. Though both stations are now closed, memories are rekindled here through the pages of *Luray and Page County.* (Harold Griffith Jr. Collection.)